Big Purpl... ...ny:

Nurturing Our Cre... ...ork,

Our Children and Ourselves

Big Purple Mommy:

Nurturing Our

Creative Work,

Our Children and

Ourselves

COLEEN HUBBARD

A PERIGEE BOOK

A Perigee Book
Published by The Berkley Publishing Group
A division of Penguin Putnam Inc.
375 Hudson Street
New York, New York 10014

First edition: March 2001

Published simultaneously in Canada.

The Penguin Putnam Inc. World Wide Web site address is
http://www.penguinputnam.com

Library of Congress Cataloging-in-Publication Data

Hubbard, Coleen.
Big purple mommy : nurturing our creative careers, our children,
and ourselves / by Coleen Hubbard.
p.   cm.
Includes index.
ISBN 0-399-52662-5
1. Working mothers.   2. Motherhood.   3. Self-realization.
4. Child development.   I. Title.
HQ759 .48.H83   2001
306.874'3—dc21   00–061181

Printed in the United States of America

10   9   8   7   6   5   4   3   2   1

For my mother and my sister—
De and Dee
—with gratitude and love.

And for big purple mommies everywhere.

Contents

PART ONE The Challenges

CHAPTER ONE
Big Purple Mommy
3

CHAPTER TWO
Looking at the Obstacles
19

CHAPTER THREE
New Vision
33

CHAPTER FOUR
The Invisibility Factor
53

CHAPTER FIVE
Your Creativity Cycle,
Your Children's Life Cycle
71

PART TWO   The Path

CHAPTER SIX
Self-Care and the Creative Woman
99

CHAPTER SEVEN
Circle of Support
113

CHAPTER EIGHT
The Time Thing
137

CHAPTER NINE
The Money Thing
157

CHAPTER TEN
Where We Create
177

CHAPTER ELEVEN
The Big Picture
195

Acknowledgments

So many people made this book possible, but none more so than Laura Shepherd, my editor extraordinaire. Thank you for your vision and tenacity.

My deepest gratitude and appreciation goes to the incredible women who shared their stories and insights, and gave the book clarity, wisdom, humor, and truth: Jahnna, Moira, Clarice, Gracie, Michele, Wendi, Lady, Maria, Aisha, Dee, Christy, and Mary.

Thank you to Larry for being my loving partner in all endeavors, and to my daughters, Allie, Natalie, and Willa, for being my daily inspiration and for allowing me to include them in my story—and for your drawing, Willa, which was the impulse for the journey, after all . . .

Part One

The Challenges

Chapter One

Big Purple Mommy

*"The Power of the womb, marvelous as it is,
does not have enough wattage
to light up a whole lifetime."*

—Anne Roiphe
Fruitful: A Real Mother in the Modern World

Behind the Scenes

As I begin this book, my three daughters end another year of school and summer is upon us. I should have been doggedly at work on the project for at least the past six weeks—taking notes, conducting interviews, making a writing plan. I should have scurried to my desk the minute my children left for school, toiling joyously with words and ideas, focused and disciplined until they returned again in the afternoon.

So what happened? Why am I late getting started, fuzzy-brained, and full of panic and dread? What became of my schedule? My plan? My life?

I'll tell you what happened, and I have a feeling you'll understand. Because if you're a woman trying to raise your children and do your creative work, it's happened to you before, and it will happen again. The plot of my story is simple: a woman loses the pulse of her creative work in the frenzy of day-to-day family life, and forgets that she had some choice in the matter, after all.

Giving In to Chaos

Since I often supplement my writing work with part-time teaching, for several years I taught drama at my oldest daughter's middle school. At the end of the term I had the happy challenge of directing the eighth grade class in a production of Oscar Wilde's *The Importance of Being Earnest.*

Now, this isn't an easy play for adults, much less for fourteen-year-old kids with their mouths full of braces, attempting to wrap their tongues around Wilde's witty and wicked British dialogue. Several students were having difficulty learning lines, we didn't have enough rehearsal time, and a couple of sullen girls who didn't like their Victorian costumes and wanted plunging necklines instead, would no longer look me in the eye. Since this was a school play and I couldn't fire the little darlings or replace them with puppets, I simply kept smiling and smiling—brighter and tighter as the days went by.

In the meantime, just to be parentally fair (a crucial concept if you have more than one child), I volunteered to help my middle daughter's fourth grade class with *their* end-of-the-year production, taking charge of movement and running a spotlight that seemed to weigh a ton. And so that my youngest wouldn't feel slighted by all of this effort, I agreed to shoot an embarrassingly amateur video of her class at work and play to show to the parents at the second grade continuation ceremony.

Now wait—don't laugh, yet. It actually gets worse! I also

had cupcakes and fruit plates to contribute to various field days and picnics, teacher appreciation gifts to buy and wrap, and thank-you cards to address to every overlooked staff member of the school. We couldn't seem to find the right dress for my oldest to wear at her middle school graduation, mainly because the girls in her class kept changing their minds about whether they would wear extremely short, baby-doll, sixties-type dresses or longer, fancier, faux-prom sorts of dresses. One thing was for certain: they would all wear very clunky platform shoes, but we couldn't find the *right* pair of clunky platform shoes!

The space in my home where I do my creative work began to seem more and more remote. To climb the short flight of stairs to the second floor seemed tantamount to climbing Everest. Dust balls grew beneath my desk and the room smelled strongly of its one and only inhabitant—the family dog. Cloudbursts of inspiration about my book came and went while I did little more than brood about how tired I was, how I would never have time to write the book, and how I no longer "had a life." To add insult to injury, my husband and I, against all sense and reason, chose those particular six weeks to have our water-damaged wood floors refinished, which meant moving two rooms of furniture into—you guessed it—my office. Even if I could have found the time to write and the courage to redefine my severely blurred boundaries, I could no longer physically reach my computer.

By the time the curtain dropped on the various plays and we found the right shoes and graduation finally happened, my body fell apart. Physically exhausted and depleted in spirit, I experienced wrenching lower back pain, abdominal distress, and interrupted sleep. The guilt I felt about abandoning the book pierced me like fishhooks, and I was suddenly filled with resentment over the endless volunteer hours I had carelessly given away in order to look like a good, willing, and fair-minded kind of mother. And I hated admitting that I was responsible for the choices that ultimately sent me to bed for a week.

Of course I could have said no to a few of the volunteer activities at my daughters' schools. I didn't have to bake anything. I didn't have to keep shopping for shoes after visiting the eighth store. I didn't have to approach the school play as though it was about to preview at a middle school but then move directly to Broadway. I certainly had a choice about when to schedule household maintenance.

I could have admitted that I was scared to begin the book and ultimately afraid of not being up to the task. I could have slowed down and looked at my issues of perfectionism and blocked creativity instead of choking my hours and days with a bizarre level of maternal self-sacrifice that had little to do with good mothering.

"*Something has to change,*" I moaned to my husband. "*My life is so completely out of balance.*"

He looked at me carefully, a smile behind his practiced *you-poor-dear* gaze. "But isn't that the subject of your book?" he asked. "How to do your creative work and be a mother? How to integrate it all? I think you're your own best audience for this."

My Own Best Audience

And so I am. My husband is right, and the truth is out. I'm really writing this book for one simple reason—*because I need to read it!*

I am my own best audience for this book, for during the past fifteen years, I have done little more than negotiate the demands and rewards of my creative life with the demands and rewards of mothering my three daughters. I have simultaneously changed diapers while talking to an editor on the phone. Volunteered at the preschool in the morning and revised a script in the afternoon. Made party favors at midnight on the eve before a Ballerina Birthday party after hurrying home from an emergency run to Kinkos and Federal Express with an overdue project.

Sometimes the double agenda makes me feel as if I have a split personality, and sometimes I just feel split in two. Here's a journal entry I made when my oldest daughter was in preschool and my middle daughter was nine months old. The children had been fighting an early fall virus, and I was waiting desperately to begin a writing fellowship with a local organization (The Rocky Mountain Women's Institute) that supplies women with studio space and a small stipend to support their creative work.

Sunday, Sept. 3, 1989: Our holiday weekend turned into a siege of illness and cancelled plans. Both girls have colds, especially Natalie, who is suffering quite a bit. We've been up with her three nights in a row—she's feverish and uncomfortable. I feel like a parental zombie, dispensing medicine, walking the floor with the baby, wiping all orifices. Feeling isolated—when you have sick kids you become near criminals to other people with children. Desperate, we tried a car ride, hoping the girls would sleep and we'd find some diversion in the scenery. Not so. Natalie fussed and Allie complained the entire time. I'm exhausted with parenthood and depressed about not writing. I feel myself gearing up for "my turn"—my semester at the Institute. So excited by the prospect of time for serious writing. Feel I can (and must) accomplish a great deal—given privacy and legitimacy.

Meeting Big Purple Mommy

I remember another particularly trying time in my life after I'd had my third child and they were in preschool, kindergarten, and second grade respectively. All I ever did was drive them to and from their schools, which, of course, all began and ended at different times. It was winter—endlessly gray and slushy—and I couldn't seem to finish the play I'd been working on for months. I'd lost my babysitter and I felt dull and lumpy as I sat in my car waiting to pick up my youngest daughter. I had fantasies of running away, of living by myself in a small, quiet, tidy place where I'd be free to write and read and rest. Every day the voice in my head cried out:

Give in! Just give in! You're a mother! You're not a writer. You live in your car. Your sweatshirt is stained. You'll never finish the play in time to submit it to the new play festival in Montana. And even if by some miracle the play is accepted, how on earth do you think you could go off to Montana for two weeks? Who would drive the carpool? Women with three young children do not get to be playwrights!

Having almost convinced myself of this, I stepped woodenly out of the car to help my preschooler into her toddler car seat. She was happy and talkative as always, filled with news of her busy day at the water table and block area. She handed me a piece of crayoned paper, which I tossed on the seat beside me, barely giving it a glance. But while stopped at a red light I took a moment to study the picture. A towering, vivid woman in a bright purple dress stood beneath a rainbow, her arms outstretched. She was taller than the trees in the picture, almost as tall as the yellow sun in the corner. She was smiling—a slightly crooked and zany smile. She looked like a woman I would want to know.

"Who's this?" I asked my daughter, thinking it was probably her teacher or a character from a story she'd read.

"You, Mommy," she answered, as though I'd asked her a particularly stupid question.

"*Me?*" I was taken by surprise. My daughter hadn't drawn a tiny, tired, colorless mommy sitting in a car with red eyes and a stained shirt. She'd drawn a *Big Purple Mommy* reaching for the sun. The kind of mother who could write plays and books and raise her children and get through the winter and maybe, *maybe* even go to Montana. Despite my fatigue and burnout and low-lying depression, my daughter still recognized and drew the part of me that was creative and larger than life and lived in the world of imagination.

This simple child's drawing (now framed and displayed over my desk) changed my perspective about what is possible for mothers who create. My daughter helped me to see that my creative self still radiates, even during fallow times. Just as I'm always a mother, even when I'm not interacting with my children, so will I always be writer—though I'm not interacting with words on a particular day. *Big Purple Mommy* made me realize how hugely important it is for me to pursue my creative work, regardless of the obstacles—not only for the necessary health of my soul but for the example it gives my daughters of how women can live authentic, complex, multilayered, and satisfying lives.

Sharing Our Stories

It isn't easy to integrate creative work and family life; in fact it's the most difficult thing I've ever done for a sustained period of time. There isn't a "right" path, or a single, simple solution for navigating the bumps and soft shoulders and sudden, heart-stopping turns. But the payoff for taking part in the journey is the fruition of your beloved creative work *and* the growth of your beloved children into creatures who value their own creativity.

The purpose of this book is to give you permission to fully emerge as a Big Purple Mommy—a woman who creates and mothers with spirit and heart and courage. The world needs more women who are willing to buck the rigid constraints of conventional domestic life and redefine the relationship between creative work and raising children. The world needs women who are able to honor both their maternal spirit *and* creative gifts, while standing taller than the trees.

The Storytellers

You're about to meet an amazing group of women who have agreed to share their experiences and insights, and serve as fellow guides on the journey. They speak candidly about the difficulty of raising children and doing creative work. They discuss their families, their relationships with partners and other mothers, and how they find support in their communities. They dispense a modicum of advice and a mountain of encouragement. They aren't "famous" women in the *People* magazine sense, but all of them are creative, intriguing women who, while mothering their children, are also struggling to stay passionately involved in their writing, painting, dancing, acting, singing, teaching, and speaking.

Though there are dozens of examples of "movie star moms" staring at us from the covers of magazines, and though these women are certainly raising their children and accomplishing their creative dreams, they don't, realistically, share our struggle. The incomparable Rosie O'Donnell articulates this beautifully in an interview with Wendy Wasserstein in *McCall's*:

> I think that every celebrity who takes credit for juggling is full of it. Look, I am very well-off. I have people who help me. I have the ability to tell Warner Brothers to build a nursery in our studio. If I want to bring my children to work, they come to work and have three meals a day with me. The studio makes its schedule around my needs. I use the power to say, "I don't want to work on a particular day because I'm going to Parker's school and I'm baking cupcakes." I have a company and I make the rules about what comes first. Most women can't do that. They're the ones who really juggle, and they deserve all the credit, not me.

(Thanks, Rosie, for speaking the truth. We feel validated, and more than a touch envious!)

Woven throughout the book are my own stories, shared with permission from my husband and daughters. Through the sorting of vivid memories, diary entries, letters, and remembered conversations, I've uncovered evidence of my maternal/creative failings and triumphs, stumbles and occasional waltz steps. Some of these stories will undoubtedly mirror your own and some may be far outside your specific realm of experience. The critical thing is to tell our stories to each other as honestly as possible—to tell them softly, loudly, with humor, with pathos, in our fear, in our courage, in our knowing.

Through the sharing of our stories, we can create a safer, more accepting and loving world for our creative selves, our mother selves, and for all of our children.

(By the way, I did go to Montana, after all. But more about that later!)

What Is *Your* Story?

Where are you in your journey of mothering, your journey of creativity?

Perhaps while you're reading this book you're also nursing your infant. And between reading and nursing, you're wondering if you'll ever get to the darkroom to develop your photographs or learn that new concerto. Will you ever dance again, paint again, get cast in another play before you're too old to play anything but grandmothers?

Perhaps your toddler is flinging her lunch at you while you wonder if you'll find a few moments today to do something creative and personally meaningful besides cleaning spaghetti off the walls. Perhaps you've finally sat down at your workspace after putting one child down to nap, only to get a call from school that your son has a "scratchy throat" and needs to come home.

Are you feeling frustrated and isolated and overwhelmed? Maybe you feel segregated from most of the other mothers you know because of your creative passion, and you no longer resemble the creative people you used to hang out with, now that you're a mother. You likely feel torn by your fierce and primal love for your children and your fierce, primal love for your creative work—and a facet of your identity that was in place perhaps decades before you became a mother. And if you work a "real" job—and I put quotes around the word carefully—where you can't or don't access your creativity, you undoubtedly feel an even greater sense that your day-to-day life is not in harmony with your soul.

Intensely wanting two seemingly disparate things simultaneously creates an unbearable tension. And when one of those things is a walking, talking, singing, yelling, crying dynamo of human need, it's tempting to turn your back on the half-finished novel or the just-started quilt and give your complete attention to little Jason or Jennifer. Our society certainly endorses this notion by telling us that our creative gifts—our calling, if you will—are merely hobbies with which to amuse ourselves when the children are napping and the soup is on the stove. A nobler, and less selfish choice, we're told, is to lead a "child-centered" life and give up the lofty and "arty" ambitions of our youth.

We're led to believe that we can't truly hold the tension of our double longing to be dedicated mothers and passionate creators. Clearly this isn't true, as the stories you're about to read bear out. But it's difficult to untangle the often negative messages we hear from family, neighbors, co-workers, the mothers in the carpool line, and even—sometimes—our well-meaning friends and partners. Not to mention the messages we give ourselves out of our guilt, fear, fatigue, and our understandable confusion about our place in the world. Hopefully, this book will help you honor your own story and give it a stronger shape, so that these destructive messages can't penetrate and endanger your singular life—which is comprised fully of children *and* creative work.

Defining "Creative Work"

There are dozens of ways to define creativity and creative work. For the purposes of this book, let's define it as:

- your passion; the work of your soul

- conjuring all of your senses toward bringing something previously unknown into the world

- directing your imagination to creative expression that is, first and foremost, for you—not a client or corporation (though most all of us, at some point, perform work for one of the above)

- the exploration of your deeply held and very individual themes, conflicts, and passions—which you then give visual, auditory, or kinesthetic life, connecting you to others and to the world at large

- the commitment to developing the creative gifts you were given through your DNA, your early environment, or your own adult searching and wandering

Now, having given you my best definition of an intangible way of being and living, I must add that *every one of us comes into the world with creative gifts of some kind.* For many (and for many reasons), the gifts can become suppressed, repressed, and eventually lost, but that's the subject of an entirely different book.

Of course there are elements of creativity in all work, but not all work is innately creative. Certainly every lawyer, doctor, realtor, and computer programmer has brilliant moments of creative thought, which result in the untangling of a complicated legal ruling, an accurate diagnosis, the sale of a property, and a new or improved product. But by and large, a client, corporation, marketplace, or institution drives these creative flashes.

In this book, you'll notice that for the most part I focus my interviews on the creative work of mothers who write, paint, dance, make music, etc. And this isn't because I value only the insights of creative artists in the more traditional venues, but because these expressive fields depend largely on internally driven emotional and psychological impulses that are captivating to explore.

Mothers who are chefs, midwives, architects, florists, and hair stylists are also highly creative people, and everything in this book applies to them as well. But choosing to focus on women involved in creative work that doesn't have the clear boundaries of "going to work" deepens the discussion at hand. Mothers who make sculpture in their garage at home are far more likely to be perceived by the outside world as women who "don't work." The woman who composes music in her dining room is far more likely to be called upon to put her work aside and drive for a school field trip than is a mother who must work a specific shift at a specific time of day.

And finally, let me say that I certainly believe being a mother in and of itself demands giant doses of creativity. To understand children, to teach, guide, and protect them requires imagination, inspiration, curiosity, intuition, problem-solving and brain-storming abilities, as well as improvisation, flexibility, bold invention, and soul-searching of a depth-defying nature. There-fore, every mother on the planet is creative—seven days a week, twenty-four hours a day for decades of her life.

But this isn't to say then, that I describe being a mother as the one true creative work of my life, for that would imply a belief in a level of control that I can't subscribe to; a belief that our children are our "products" or "clients" and that through our own hard work and sheer dedication we can mold the "clay" into our vision of perfection. This discounts our children's own natures and passions, decisions and wisdom. It leaves little room for them to become the artists of their own souls—a right they are inherently born to.

The creative work of our own souls must not be confused with creatively raising children, or raising creative children. For if we are led to believe that our children must become our creative work, then we must also believe that when our children grow up and leave us, our creativity leaves us, too.

This is a vision too chilling and forsaken to even imagine. In order to sustain ourselves on the Big Purple Mommy journey, we must hold our children in one hand and our creative gifts in the other, palms open and uplifted, recognizing that each hand holds something of immense, indescribable value, knowing that each hand tends the other, and that the weight in each hand will shift and change every day of our lives. Most importantly, both hands, while separate, extend from our two arms, which are connected to our body, which house our heart and soul.

To Contemplate

• Do you have any visual reminders of yourself doing your creative work or expressing your creative self? A photograph, or a drawing, perhaps? If not, think about asking your partner, friend, or child to take/make one of you. Display it in a prominent space and make a point of looking at it several times a day—especially when you're most feeling like "just a mom."

• Close your eyes and think about your two hands, one holding your child(ren) and one holding your creative work. Is the weight in one hand different from the other? How long has it felt like that? What possibilities exist for lightening the weight in that heavier hand, just for today?

Chapter Two

Looking at the Obstacles

*"Women today, trying to compose lives that
will honor all their commitments and still
express all their potentials with a certain
unitary grace, do not have an easy task."*

—Mary Catherine Bateson
Composing A Life

The obstacles to accomplishing creative work while successfully raising children are different for everyone. Each woman featured in this book has a slightly different view on what makes the combination so difficult. For many, the lack of time is the biggest factor—the inability to carve out any significant personal time not only to create, but also to daydream and ponder and find the nearly invisible seeds of an idea. The time factor is so daunting that I've devoted an entire chapter to it later in the book.

For some women, the cultural stereotyping of both artists and mothers makes forging a true identity almost impossible. (I have to tell you that in my favorite local bookstore, books on "creativity" are followed directly by books on "depression." I know it's an alphabetical coincidence, but I savor the irony anyway!)

For others, the negative messages about our creative gifts instilled in us as children continue to haunt us as adults. And for a large group of us, our perfectionist tendencies—the need to score a perfect ten as mothers and in our creative work—sometimes leave us too depleted to accomplish much of anything.

For women whose creative work involves expensive materials, finding the extra money in an already tight budget can be an ongoing (and draining) dilemma. It's hard to save upwards of a hundred dollars for a large canvas when you have a child in braces and your car needs a new transmission.

And finally, for some women who are single parents, and for some women living with non-supportive partners, achieving creative dreams often takes a back seat to the day-to-day workload of raising a family. (Look for a longer discussion in Chapter Seven on creating a support system.)

But now let's delve into some of our culture's beliefs about mothers and creativity.

The Creative Identity vs. the Mother Identity

Our culture holds a dim view of creative work. You don't have to dig very deep to uncover example after example of famous creative people suffering from depression, madness, alcoholism, drug abuse, and a rich assortment of shocking, dangerous, antisocial, and deeply adolescent behavior. We all know the stories of poets who put their heads in the oven, painters who cut off their own ears, and dancers who develop frightening eating disorders. No wonder it's hard for women to blend these images with the overly idealized picture of American motherhood that our society seems never to tire of. It is a challenge to find positive examples of creative people, much less creative women who also succeed at motherhood. So, it's not surprising that the idea of a woman possessing both of these (highly stereotypical) identities seems particularly incongruous: imagine cutting off your ear in a bout of artistic frustration and then having to go pick up the kids from soccer practice with a plate of homemade cookies beside you on the seat of the mini-van!

In her absorbing book, *Fruitful: A Real Mother in the Modern World*, Anne Roiphe expounds on the conflict between the creative and maternal identity:

> Of course it may be that great art requires a kind of monomania, an absorption so intense that children would be interferences, beside the point. It may be that great art is made by men and women who are exempt from the pull of ordinariness. The artists we admire may all be half mad. I doubt they have any choice in the matter. Who would choose to be an artist when they could be just a man or a woman living an ordinary life? Possibly I say that because I'm a woman lacking ambition. Possibly I say this because I have seen so many lives consumed in the pursuit of great art. That passion is not unconnected to alcoholism and madness and while great art comforts us all, its creators are frequently moral freaks. Ambition is certainly not an exclusively male characteristic but in its extreme, a desire to challenge the gods, it may be a condition incompatible with child care.

Luckily, most of us aren't trying to "challenge the gods" or even make "great" art. Most of us are merely aiming for more polish and proficiency in our creative work, and more time to focus our ideas before one or more child needs our attention. But Roiphe's point rings true, nonetheless: monomania and the idea of becoming a moral freak is largely incongruent with our maternal identity and our "ordinary" lives.

Meet Maria

Maria Katzenbach is a single mother who lives with her ten-year-old son in the Denver metro area. An innately dramatic woman with a rich, theatrical voice, Maria captures the immediate attention of all that meet her. Besides being a published author, she also teaches, makes collage, and is trained as a facilitator for a genre of interactive theatre called Playback Theatre. Here's what she has to say about how our society perceives creativity, and she says it not with anger, but with quiet acceptance of its truth:

> The message from the dominant culture is that to be creative is to be sick; to be creative is to be at risk for manic depression; to be creative, especially if you're a writer, is to look at misery. To be creative is to be neurotic. Creative people are incapable of living in a "normal" family and having a "normal family life."
>
> The message is that you will be a lousy parent if you're an artist. No question about it. Unless, of course, you're successful. The culture will forgive anybody anything if you make a lot of money.

It's no surprise that so many of us put down the paintbrush and pick up the baby. With such bad press, what sane person would choose the supposed torment of the creative identity—especially when the identity of the "good mother" is so likely to garner high praise from every corner? Would you rather be described as flaky, neurotic, twisted, odd, selfish, and narcissistic, or devoted, self-sacrificing, dependable, cheerful, wise, and nurturing?

Enviably, Maria manages to buck the stereotypes of both artist and mother and live in a way that combines the best of both passions. She is neither the selfish artist nor the selfless mother, but something completely unique. And she's determined to model a more positive way for her son to engage in creativity:

> For me, motherhood and creativity merged into one when I realized that if I did not show my son how to do what it takes to realize a gift, then I was failing at probably the most important gift I could give him as a mother.

Messages from Childhood

Sadly, some of us heard and absorbed negative messages about our creativity during childhood. When we were young and vulnerable and so needy of our family's approval, we began to get the clear idea that to be creative wasn't necessarily a good or valued trait. We knew that our creative longings stirred up strong feelings in our family, but we weren't exactly sure *why*.

In my particular family of origin, what was most valued was compliance, sportsmanship, conformity, and acting for the "good of the family" rather than for the development of the individual. I craved privacy as a child, but when I tried to slip off to my room to write in my diary, or daydream on my bed, I was deemed "selfish." If I called attention to myself by being dramatic and exuberant, I was called one of several stinging nicknames, including *Queenie*, because I presumably acted like a queen, or *Sarah Bernhardt*, presumably because I overacted, and acted badly. When I clung fiercely to my need for a dark, quiet, room in which to sleep and dream, I was teased about wanting to live like a rat or a bat.

I'm certain I wasn't an easy child for my parents to raise. I lived in the world of my own imagination, endlessly reading and scrawling melodramatic poems in various little diaries and note-books. I danced in the living room to old recordings of Broadway musicals, imagining myself performing at Lincoln Center, no less. I directed backyard plays and became easily frustrated when the neighbor kids didn't share my "artistic vision" for a particular project. I had a high need for emotional expressiveness in a family that was emotionally subdued.

To escape, I often fantasized that I came from a different family altogether—and that they would eventually come back and claim me (when they were finished with their world theatrical tour, or escaped from being imprisoned behind the Iron Curtain for writing controversial novels!).

But despite the fact that I surely drove my family crazy, the message I received in childhood was that I was somehow "bad" or "flawed" and that to withdraw into creativity was "selfish;" it didn't serve others and it just plain looked rude. Of course, as an adult I've come to realize that both my parents are people who had their own creative tendencies discouraged during child-hood. They were raised in an era that supported the notion that children should be "seen and not heard" and that artistic pursuits were a waste of time and energy on the difficult road of life. My father, though untrained, can play the harmonica and guitar and has a talent for drawing. My mother likes to sing and write and was very involved in theatre during her high school years. That I inherited the creative gene from people who were never allowed to access it themselves is a bittersweet realization.

And even today, though my parents (and my mother in particular) are now big supporters of my creative work, I still suffer a brief, thirty-five-year-old twinge of guilt each time I choose to remove myself from family life and seek shelter in my quiet, private workspace.

For just a second, on my way up the steps, I hear the word *selfish* and shudder.

Meet Gracie

When Gracie Carr began to show creative urges as a child, her parents weren't sure what to think. She thinks back to her early desires and remarks:

When it became clear that mine was a passion beyond their wildest dreams, that I wanted to sing and act in shows, there was a lot of reluctance on their part. They thought show business was evil. I remember watching Merv Griffin, with all those show people talking about themselves. And my parents would say, "Why in Sam Hill do you want to listen to those people?" But they consumed me, because they were living the life I wanted. It was a struggle.

Luckily, Gracie didn't heed the early messages she heard, or give up the struggle. Today, she is an accomplished musician, actress, teacher *and* the mother of a college-aged stepdaughter and a younger daughter named Johanna. Whether interacting with the students she teaches at St. Mary's Academy, singing solos in her church choir, acting in commercials and plays, or composing at the piano, Gracie exudes a warmth, a rich spiritual nature, and a zest for life that is inspirational. It probably won't surprise you to hear that after the struggle of her own childhood, an important part of her adult life is devoted to helping young people discover and tap their creative gifts. (She recently took twenty high school choir students to sing in Rome, and lived to show me the pictures!)

Daydreaming and Diaper Changing

While authentic creativity is rarely an act of selfishness, it seems that many creative people are innately wired with a certain amount of what our culture calls "artistic temperament." To be creative is to sometimes need privacy and quiet. To be creative is to sometimes be so distracted by our own inner visions that nothing else permeates. To be creative is to sometimes be involved in daydreaming instead of "doing." To be creative is to sometimes be a non-conformist in both our yearnings and our lifestyle.

However—and this is the crux of the matter—*being a mother requires us to stay fully present in the maternal rather than artistic temperament.* We can't daydream while watching a toddler play in a busy park. We can't be distracted when helping a second-grader practice reading. We can't often find quiet and privacy in the midst of family life. *For the well being of our children, we feel we must be unfalteringly consistent, reliable, present and attentive, while our creative work calls us to wander half-dazed inside our own head.*

The woman you're about to meet skillfully describes the distraction dilemma.

Meet Lady

Lady McCrady is a fine arts painter who lives in a seaside town in eastern Connecticut, with her husband and school-aged son and daughter. High-spirited and quirky, she was once part of Andy Warhol's art circle in New York. She has a roster of gallery showings to her credit, and was once featured in *Interview* magazine. But in the years since having children, she claims:

> The importance of what I do is less obvious to other people. I appear to have dropped out. My résumé is quite empty of public exhibitions and multiple accolades. Strangers used to know my work—now only people who know me do.

Expounding on the daydream/diaper dilemma, she notes:

> I'm too creative with everything, so very practical things that could be done quickly, simply take forever to do. My mind wanders all the time to painting or shapes or space, and the way things fit in it; or the colors of things, no matter where I look. The children say, Mom, do you hear me? When I don't answer, it's because I'm seeing things, or re-arranging space in my head, or thinking through a situation with different colors.

So many of the women I've spoken to describe distraction as the experience of having one eye on their children and the other focused inward on their creative thoughts. We feel somehow guilty over this, as if we should be required to always keep a sharp, penetrating laser beam pointed at our child's every movement. I wonder if perhaps it isn't usually enough to have *one* strong eye on duty, knowing that our children can feel smothered and trapped by our attention if we never let our thoughts wander from them.

Our Need to Be Perfect

Many (though certainly not all) of us have perfectionist tendencies that interfere with our ability to balance motherhood and creativity. We feel driven to excel at parenting, even with the impossibly high and often inaccurate standards of measurement set for us by our culture. We feel pressure to excel at our creative work—this time setting impossibly high standards for ourselves. We feel we should somehow be a combination of Georgia O'Keefe and Donna Reed (or her more current counterpart, Martha Stewart). Since Americans seem to value competence and results over exploration and process, we feel we don't measure up in our work, or in our families.

We are so racked with guilt over our imperfections that we sometimes feel frozen and empty, unable to "do anything right."

Meet Jahnna

After just a few moments in Jahnna Beecham's presence, I always find myself wiping tears of laughter from my eyes as she regales me with wild tales of her personal endeavors and her often chaotic family life. Like any truly funny person, her humor is derived from the details of her own life and the story she is living.

Jahnna lives in Oregon, with her husband, Malcolm, and school-aged children, Skye and Dash. A prolific writer, she has co-authored eighty-three books with her husband, including their popular children's series, *The Jewel Kingdom*. And while this sounds like (and is) an enormous amount of creative success, Jahnna is quick to point out that it doesn't necessarily mean that she enjoys financial freedom or the security of knowing what her next project will be. (We'll follow her financial story later in the book.)

In the past several years, she has begun to develop a new facet of her creative life by producing and directing film, and this year she and Malcolm formed Starcatcher Press to publish their own books.

But Jahnna also knows the pitfalls of being a perfectionist mother/creator:

Since the birth of our children, we've written books and plays, Malcolm has gone back to acting again, and I've continued my directing career. So, more things are happening, creatively, but the stress level is incredible. My biggest concern has been how not to take the stress out on the kids. There are some nights when I go into their room and they're asleep. I whisper, "I'm so sorry! I'm such a bad mother!"

And I constantly have to say, "Okay. I know the book or project is due. I was going to make the Federal Express deadline, but I promised the kids I'd go to school and carve pumpkins." It's really hard to just think, okay, the world won't stop if my project is a day late. I mean, we always make our deadlines. Once, in a snowstorm in Oklahoma, we drove from FedEx box to FedEx box, looking for a truck that was still driving so we could make a deadline. We made the deadline—only to discover that the editor we were sending it to had gone on vacation!

Clearly, if you know Jahnna at all, you know she's a terrific mother, and the consummate professional regarding her creative work. But in her own mind, she never *quite* measures up in either direction.

In her funny and exquisitely truthful book on parenting called *I'm Okay . . . You're a Brat*, Susan Jeffers takes aim at the way our society peddles guilt to mothers:

> Never was there a time of such pervasive guilt in women when it comes to the raising of their children. Men experience a touch of guilt themselves, but nothing compared to the guilt women take on with the birth of a child. One might think mother-guilt just comes with the territory; in fact mother-guilt, in the extreme form it is today, is a relatively new phenomenon. It has been created by a society that has gone slightly mad with the raising of its children.

Jeffers goes on to point the finger at various "guilt peddlers" including: society in general, friends and family, strangers, teachers, the media, childcare experts, and our children themselves. She warns us to ignore the guilt-peddlers and pay attention to our own instincts about parenting. Finally, she lists some important beliefs of happy parents, including my favorite:

> They know they are entitled to pursue other interests and have a full and balanced life. By enjoying many things in their own life, they are enjoying their children as well.

Committing Once Again

I take great solace in Jeffers's words. But I have much work to do in banishing the guilt-peddlers from my life. At least once a week I call my husband at work and confess to him through my tears that I'm a terrible mother, a pathetic excuse for a writer, an absent friend, a loathsome spouse, and an all-around despicable human being. I recount my "bad mommy" moments and my "failed artist" moments until I'm purged, or until my husband gently reminds me that he's trying to do his own creative work, and could I please get a grip and maybe go take a walk, or at least take a few deep breaths.

I tell him that I've risked brain cancer by calling him on the cell phone on the way to pick up our daughters after school, and by the way, could he please pick up groceries on the way home because the cupboards are bare and my book is unfinished, and there's a pretty scary leak in the dining room ceiling.

These are the moments when I look, once again, at the *Big Purple Mommy* drawing above my desk, take that deep breath, and try to renew my commitment to the journey.

To Contemplate

- What's the biggest personal obstacle to doing your creative work while raising your children? Is it time? Money? Cultural expectations? Old messages from childhood? Your own perfectionism? Guilt? A combination of several of these? Can you sift through these issues and identify the area that's most troublesome for you? Can you name it and then begin to think of how to do your creative work in spite of it?

Wise Words

"Have a business card printed with what you intend to do when you have more time, as the children get

older. Your intentions will guide you and keep you on track. We moved from New York when the children were small, which was great for our family's lifestyle, less good for my professional life. My card proved that I have a purpose in life, that I am somebody (since my new acquaintances didn't know that!) and they reacted by expecting a certain level from me, when I was feeling my most frazzled and lackluster."
—Lady McCrady

"Get up early in the morning and don't talk to anybody—preserve the Dream State. If I'm into my artwork, the dreams are really important, because that's where a lot of my imagery comes from. And if I'm working intensely on a book, usually problems are solved in dreaming. So that moment, the moment of getting up, getting dressed, facing the world—you have to be careful not to lose the dreams. Just driving—the school dropoff circle—can undo everything."
—Maria Katzenbach

"A lot of times I get really good ideas in church. I think it's the quiet. Something's going on, but I can open up to the quiet and actually get some creative work done—with my daughter right next to me."
—Gracie Carr

"My best advice—hire a house cleaner!"
—Jahnna Beecham

Chapter Three

New Vision

"We live in a culture that has left the
mother's experience, the mother's
perspective, the mother's power in the
shadows."

—Naomi Ruth Lowinsky, Ph.D.
Stories From the Motherline

First, Some Good News

Now that we've defined and described some of the obstacles involved in raising our children and doing our creative work, it's time to look at the flip side of the dilemma. I think it's important to illuminate a fairly universal truth, and that is that *despite the overwhelming and inherent difficulties, our experience of being a mother feeds and nourishes our creative souls.* Being mothers gives depth to our work and to our understanding of the world. The problems of personal time, creative identity, money and priorities may never go away, but they don't diminish the gifts of wonder, laughter, and perspective that our children bring to us.

Overall, the women I interviewed felt strongly that having children freed their spirits, unleashed hidden forms of creativity, and opened their hearts to new levels of love and understanding. This is especially true for women who have been mothers long enough to look back and take stock of the positive changes that have occurred since bringing children into their lives. If you're a brand new mother, or the mother of an infant or toddler, you may have a different perspective—and who could blame you? It definitely takes a significant number of miles on the motherhood journey to begin to understand all of the enormous shifts occurring in your life.

I think the best news for all of us is that so many of the women I spoke to during the process of writing this book actually discovered their true creative calling in tandem with becoming mothers. Others discovered that the very subject of children and mothers became a compelling creative theme, and some radically changed the form and content of their earlier work. Sometimes a new creative vision seems to emerge from the chaos of motherhood, bound by the powerful experience of falling in love with our children. (This experience, we should note, counters the widely proclaimed myth that having children depletes and drains us of our creativity.)

My own vision changed dramatically after becoming a mother—literally and creatively. The literal part is that soon after the birth of my second child, I experienced a sudden decrease in my vision, which resulted in a stronger correction in my contact lenses. Though I initially panicked and thought I was going blind, my doctor explained that vision changes aren't unusual at all and fall into the same category as increased shoe size, thinning hair, and other post-pregnancy occurrences.

This was comforting news, but I still don't discount the potent coincidence of needing a new lens with which to view the world at exactly the same moment my world had been split open once again.

And as I track the evolution of my writing over the past fifteen years, it's clear that motherhood has left its figurative imprint on my creative vision, too. Once narrowly focused on writing about the drama of contemporary adult life and relationships, having children nudged me into shifting my creative focus to include other generations, other kinds of relationships, other periods of history, and deeper, more enduring themes. I became interested in how individuals relate within various kinds of families. I wondered about the real experience of my own childhood as I watched my children grow. I researched how other women with children made their lives work, within different kinds of cultures.

Eventually, after years of reading children's books to my daughters I branched into that field myself, leaving playwriting behind for a time to write books about the world of boys and girls (and quite a few horses and dogs!). Having children gave me the kind of writing education I couldn't have found in an academic writing program: I learned firsthand how kids think and talk, what makes them laugh and shiver and worry and grin. And then, as my children grew older and I mused about the poignant and hilarious stories that came out of our day-to-day life, I turned to personal essays as a way of both documenting and understanding my children as complex individuals in a complex world.

I sometimes wonder what subjects and themes I would have been drawn to in my writing without the frame of motherhood in my life. Though the adults-only world is compelling, and ripe with endless possibilities, I have a sense that my writing would have become predictable and stale, and a bit too narcissistic.

The woman you're about to meet also experienced a creative

about-face following the birth of her first child, and entirely changed the direction of her life.

Meet Christy

Christy Cutler is a dancer/choreographer who has been teaching children to dance for nearly two decades. She and her business partner manage their own company called Children's Dance Place, where children from infants to age ten explore creative movement and learn the joy of bodies in motion. To be around the lovely and expressive Christy is to envy any child fortunate enough to spend an hour in her studio. (Indeed, many mothers bring their children to her mother/toddler class and have such a good time that they refuse to graduate, even when their children are old enough to move on to other classes!) With her sparkling eyes and infectious laugh, Christy builds instant community wherever she is.

But Christy never really planned on a career in dance, even though she had been dancing and performing since she was thirteen. She graduated from college with a degree in Italian, and spent the decade before having children as a researcher and counselor at a center for abused children. She explains:

I believe that my creative work started around the birth of my children. I had always dabbled in dance, taken dance classes—but I'd never made it a real focus in my life until after having children. I knew that once I had children, it would no longer fit for me to have a career where I had full-time child care and worked full time. It just didn't make any sense to me, and emotionally, after having Anna, I wouldn't have done anyone much good for a while.

When her daughter was three, Christy and a fellow mother and friend "trotted our daughters way out to the suburbs to the one school that taught the type of dance we wanted—creative movement." Apparently all was fine—for a few weeks—until both women realized that *they* could teach the same kind of dance, but in the city, closer to where they lived.

> That's how my dance career got started. Something in me got freed up after having children. It just allowed that part of me, which had always been there, to come to the fore. There was that softening, that readiness . . .

It's interesting to contemplate that becoming a mother can generate both the "softening" of a woman's spirit, but also the sharpening of her creative focus. Somewhere between those seemingly opposite poles is a large, mostly unexplored country where many of us live our lives. And perhaps the "readiness" Christy mentions is the singularly rich time following the birth or adoption of our children that paves the way for us to give birth to our own creative gifts.

Like Christy, Moira Keefe experienced that same creative readiness emerging after the birth of her first daughter.

Meet Moira

Called simply "Keefe" by her large circle of women friends, Moira lives in a suburb of San Diego with her husband (whom she comically refers to as Spouse) and two daughters she calls Scoop and Rocky. A natural comedian and storyteller, Moira writes and performs solo theatre pieces that have delighted audiences across the country, as well as in Canada, Ireland, and New Zealand.

With searing wit and unflagging honesty, Moira writes about children, family, and marriage in a decidedly unsentimental fashion. Imagine a woman with the physical comedy style of Lucille Ball, the Long Island–tinged voice of Rosie O'Donnell, and the slightly twisted world view of Roseanne, and you have Moira Keefe—onstage and in "real" life. Once headed for a more traditional career in acting, Moira's creative work took a completely different direction after giving birth to her first child.

I became focused. Because I became a mother, I wrote my first show, called LIFEAFTERBIRTH. In a way, becoming a mother gave me the confidence to write—or maybe once I became a mother, I lost my mind because I was hanging around the house full time! Anyway, that first show was pretty well received. Then, when I moved to Denver, I found my girlhood diaries, which became the basis for my second show, called LIFE BEFORE SEX.

Since her first solo piece inspired by her initiation into motherhood, Moira has added several other popular shows to her repertoire, including: *Staying Married: Life Before the Crisis*; and her new piece about the shadow side of life in suburbia, *The Crisis: There's a Rat in My Three-Car Garage.*

Through motherhood, Moira not only found her voice and her confidence, but found her subject matter as well—one that unfolds as she moves through her own life, and her children grow up. And since raising children can provide an endless source of content, it's easy to imagine all of the plots still ahead for Moira to explore: sending her daughter to high school, the empty-nest syndrome, the hellish wedding that ends up fine in the end, becoming a sassy grandmother—you get the idea!

*   *   *

For Jahnna Beecham, whom we met in the previous chapter, having children caused her to re-examine the subject matter she's willing to explore in her writing.

No More Scary Stories

Among Jahnna's many published books is a series of horror stories for older kids, including the best-selling *Scared Stiff*, which is set in a mortuary. Though Jahnna enjoyed writing the books at the time and depended on them for income, as a mother she found herself having second thoughts about the genre.

During the course of a year (1997–98), Jahnna and her husband, Malcolm, contributed a series of weekly parenting columns for *Sesame Street Parent's Online*, sharing humorous and poignant installments from their daily family life. In a column called "Nightmare on Oak Street," Jahnna explains how having children made her vow never again to write scary books depicting monsters and beasts.

> We weren't really aware of the impact these stories could have on kids until we had two of our own . . . When Skye was four and Dash was almost seven, we were hired to ghostwrite a scary book for a well-known children's author. Since the language was simple and the chapters short, I decided I'd try out a few chapters on the kids while they were in the bathtub. Big mistake.

Jahnna goes on to describe how frightened her kids were over the part in the book where a shadow on the wall becomes a monster. Her son chastised her for writing such a "terrible" story, and her daughter had nightmares that very night about the evil shadow appearing in her bedroom. The next day Jahnna alerted her publisher that she was finished with the scary book business.

This incident prompted Jahnna and Malcolm to create a new book series of their own called *The Jewel Kingdom*, which features princesses and unicorns, and a friendly dragon or two, but absolutely no monsters. The ultimate outcome of this story is that Jahnna's creative focus changed forever because her children gave her a new vision of what she wanted to contribute to children's fiction.

Ironically, other mothers unearth their creative calling by going deep into the world of shadows and facing down their personal "monsters." Allow me to introduce you to a woman who eventually found her voice after the devastating experience of losing a child.

Meet Dee

When Dee Paddock was just a few days away from giving birth to her first child, the baby inexplicably stopped moving. Though friends tried to comfort her by assuring her that fetal movement often slows in the final stage of pregnancy, she knew something was wrong. And then her doctor confirmed her worst fear in a hospital ultrasound—her tiny daughter's heart was no longer beating. Even more difficult than digesting this sudden tragedy was the trauma of having to give birth that day to a stillborn child, with her heartbroken husband at her side.

After Dee and her husband, John, held their daughter, Sara, wrapped in a hospital receiving blanket, family members gathered in the cramped hospital room. Compassionate nurses and social workers explained how important it was to the grieving process to name the baby, hold the baby, take pictures of her, and tell her she was loved and would be missed. The tears that flowed that bleak December afternoon were gut-wrenching and unstoppable.

How, you may be wondering, could anything *creative* possibly come from such a horrendous loss? Well, it didn't happen overnight, to be sure. And it wasn't an easy journey. But the mysterious pull of parental longing led Dee and her husband to adopt three children from Korea—an infant daughter first, and two preschool-aged sons several years later. During this time, she returned to school for a masters degree in counseling, spending several strenuous years in night classes while working at an adoption agency during the day. After setting up a private practice specializing in adoption issues, Dee became a trainer and facilitator in the adoption field, and is now a widely sought-after national speaker.

> My creative work is speaking and presenting. I present workshops, keynote speeches, and training for adoption agencies, both public and private. It's creative in that a certain aspect of it is performance. Speaking is definitely a performance. And I creatively integrate stories from my own life, and family to enliven the research, clinical theory and practice.
>
> My creative work came directly from the stillborn death of my daughter, Sara, and from the adoption of my three children from Korea. I didn't even know what I wanted to be doing "when I grew up" until Sara died and we entered

the adoption process. Then I realized there was this bizarre little world and no one was talking about it—telling the truth about it. By speaking about it, I have figured out my story. And every time I tell my story it becomes more known to me.

No woman should have to endure the loss of a child in order to find her creative voice. And yet for Dee, that unfathomable loss is forever entwined with her discovery of her path, her passion, and her significant creative gifts. Every time Dee speaks to an audience and shares her stories, her voice honors the memory of her daughter, and the singular lives of her three other children.

And . . . the Not-So Good News

Clearly, for many of us the experience of becoming mothers so profoundly rocks our world that it not only changes the very essence of who we are, but changes our creative work, too. My own writing "voice" deepened after having children, becoming more personal and textured, more concerned with a core theme of women's identities. This is the good news, to be sure. *But the bad news is that upon becoming a mother, my own identity underwent such enormous changes that the person I was before nearly disappeared before my eyes.*

Motherhood USA

Some of this disappearing act has to do with the sad fact that motherhood in our country is an isolating experience. It takes you out of the commerce of the world, because very few institutions, events, or public places welcome women with children.

We are frowned upon, frowned *at*, and made to feel like a barely tolerated nuisance. Once, when I was trying to put two small children and six bags of groceries into my car, two well-dressed women walked past me, gave me undisguised scowls, and said, "Oh, look—another *breeder*."

It didn't occur to them, I suppose, that I was in the midst of writing a play that had a fierce grip on me, that I was *at work* on a project that, when finished, would be personally important and publicly lauded. To them, high heels clicking, I was less than human, some substandard female species involved in the embarrassing display of *breeding*. Looking back on that encounter, I recall, ironically, that the play I was writing was titled *Motherload*—about a woman trying to come to terms with motherhood, who feels constantly bombarded by disembodied voices. A chorus of three actors plays these uncensored voices that endlessly spew out their judgments, opinions, advice and warnings about raising children. The two women from the parking lot encounter could have stepped directly out of my play!

It's chilling to think that this kind of harsh judgment is leveled at mothers by members of our very own sex who have undoubtedly experienced harassment of some kind in their own lives. And it doesn't stop there; we also have to deal with the special brand of judgment cast on mothers by *men*. I've found that men criticize mothers as often as other women, though perhaps in a less confrontational way. Sometimes it's merely a blank look, a raised eyebrow, or as in an encounter Christy Cutler describes, the painful act of being entirely dismissed.

When she was a brand-new mother and no longer working at her previous job, Christy remembers going out in the world with her husband:

> People would ask what I do and I'd tell them I was a mother and home with a baby. And people would literally turn

around and walk away! Especially men—because they'd have nothing to say to me. They'd look at me like, "That's all you have to say for yourself!" Sometimes I feel I started teaching dance just so I'd have something to say!

Every mother has horror stories of the disapproving looks and comments hurled at her by strangers while trying to nurse an infant in a restaurant, discretely change a diaper where no facilities exist, calm a toddler in the midst of a full-blown tantrum, or fit into a voting booth with a double stroller and bulging diaper bag. Consequently, many mothers of very young children find themselves staying home more often than they'd like—it's easier on the ego, if not the spirit.

For me, those years with small children were hothouse years. I breathed the moist, cloistered air of baby food and diaper pails, tripped over small plastic toys, and tried to keep step with a slow-ticking clock that was out of sync with the world going by outside my kitchen window, and the creative work fermenting in my soul. To have been spared the unkind words and diffident looks of strangers might have made all the difference.

On the Fringe of the Already "Fringed"

Unwelcome in the world, and feeling profoundly voiceless, women with children try desperately to form small bands of other mothers who meet at playgrounds, shopping malls, and in each other's homes. There, with safety in numbers, these groups find the modern day equivalent of "tea and sympathy"—or what I call Cappuccino and Company. Such groups can be a wonderful haven, offering support, advice, companionship, and huge doses of laughter. But they can also, at times, serve to further isolate mothers who are trying to stay involved in their creative work.

Cappuccino and Company

Over the years, I was a sometime member of several different, loosely organized playgroups, which met weekly in homes around the neighborhood. We would bring our babies and all of our gear, and maybe a plate of muffins to share. And though this all smacks faintly of our own mothers and their "Coffee Klatches" of the 50's and 60's, there was a big difference. Almost every mother at the gatherings I attended were women who had left long and productive careers to raise children, and though they sometimes referred nostalgically to their days in law and advertising and teaching and finance, these women were there to talk babies!

And talk babies we did. Talk and talk and talk. Whose baby was not yet crawling. Whose had endured three courses of antibiotics and still had that nagging ear infection. Who had visited which preschool and *did you know that they didn't even wash their hands before snack there!* We quoted articles by pediatricians and educators and toy companies. We held and burped and wiped and sipped until the coffee was long gone and it was time to head home for our children's morning naps. It was almost as if by engaging in the endless baby chatter we could have the faintly remembered experience of having a voice!

I liked those gatherings, make no mistake. They filled a void in my isolated mother life and made the clock tick just a bit faster, if even for a morning. And I met some wonderful women. But those mornings also, in a very particular way, made me feel even more lonely and isolated. Because while I held and burped, and sipped and nodded, I was always thinking about my play or my book, and how much work I might accomplish during that brief but blessed afternoon nap. Would I get that scene written? Would I have time to make some notes? Why couldn't I get the beginning of Act Two down on paper when I'd played it all out in my head for days? Why couldn't we stop talking about toilet training already? Was I the only one not blissfully happy and completely contented as a mother? How was it possible to be in a crowd of my familiars and feel so lonely and disengaged?

Telling the Truth

For me, the greatest difficulty about the Cappuccino and Company gatherings, especially when I was a first-time mother, was the unspoken and collective agreement that we wouldn't speak the truth about what we were living. We wouldn't admit that we were tired and depressed and isolated. We wouldn't talk about the parts of staying home with children that felt over-whelmingly difficult and unfair. We never talked about how we were too tired to have sex with our partners, how we sometimes didn't feel loving toward our own children, how we hadn't had time to have lunch with a friend or read the paper or trim our raggedy fingernails. (One day I suddenly realized that with three children, I had a combined total of sixty toenails and fingernails to trim on a weekly basis—not to mention my own personal twenty!)

Pretending I was managing it all and loving it, too, was one of the hardest parts of being a new mother.

To Not Be Cast Out

From the moment we bring a child into our life, women quickly figure out how important it is to perpetuate the image that we're fine, our children are thriving, *and life just couldn't be any better*. We go to great lengths to project the impression that we're good mothers, we have splendid children, peaceful homes, supportive partners, satisfying friendships and well-tended cuticles.

What's the deep down, gut-wrenching reason for the façade? I think that for mothers to admit to anything less, to give voice to anything less is to risk judgment from other mothers. And the result of being deemed unfit by fellow mothers is to be cast out of the tribe and to be truly alone in our already isolated experience of mothering.

To further complicate the dynamic of these gatherings was a second unspoken rule followed with strict adherence: we wouldn't speak of ourselves as individuals, but only as mothers. This meant, then, that we didn't share anything too personal, or quirky, or real about who we were. I didn't talk about the play I was writing precisely because *I was writing a play about the really hard parts of being a mother!* How could I reveal this fact to women who seemed, on the outside at least, to be managing motherhood so happily? I couldn't imagine how they might respond to the main character in my play making the following confession to her sister during a very difficult time:

MARTA: (to her sister) Just wait until you have kids and realize you'll never be happy again. (Pause) I mean, one night right after I had Barney—I'm sitting in the rocking chair gazing at his little wrinkled monkey face, and all of a sudden he makes this awful grimace, like he's really in pain or something? And I start to panic, and have flashes of brain tumors and cancer and spinal meningitis. And it was just gas. But I knew at that moment—at that precise moment—that I would never be free to be happy again. Because of him, and the responsibility of taking care of him, and the worry of what could happen to him, and what his life would be like and was he happy and did he need something and was I doing it right? And about a month later I read this article in the newspaper about this medical study where the researchers concluded that maybe as many as ten percent of crib deaths were not accidental? Meaning that the babies were smothered? And I could almost understand that—that impulse to put the pillow over this little creature's head—just so you could have back one more chance to be happy . . .

Luckily, when the play had a local production, many of the women who attended actually thanked me for writing the truth and offered their own stories of mother love in the trenches—even some of the women from my neighborhood! I felt a certain amount of personal triumph in having survived the scary experience of trying to shed some light on the reality of being a mother. *Motherload* sold out every night, and was later remounted in a second theatre for another run—which says less about my writing talent than it does about our need for a little dose of the truth on the subject.

One of my favorite books that tells the truth about motherhood is *The Mother Knot* by Jane Lazarre. Over the years, I've given away dozens of copies to friends and my own edition is tattered and wrinkled from use. In the following passage, Lazarre talks about her feelings following the birth of her son:

I felt I should never have had a baby. If anyone had told me what it would be like, I might have saved my life in time. Who was this immensely powerful person, screaming unintelligibly, sucking my breast until I was in a state of fatigue the likes of which I had never known? Who was he and by what authority had he claimed the right to my life? I would never be a good mother.

Over the years, of course, I have met many extraordinary women who break easily through these group-imposed boundaries and tell the raw truth about motherhood and everything else (though usually in pairs and away from the scrutiny of the group). The women interviewed in this book certainly risk the truth. But it's still a mystery to me how the Big Silence around motherhood perpetuates itself in playgroups and on playgrounds across the country. No other group of people I know of who share a common identity are so willing to sanitize the reality of their job. Have you ever listened to a couple of attorneys talk about their work and shed all pretense within a couple of minutes? How about teachers? Medical personnel? High-tech execs, and low-paid clerks?

And let's not leave writers out of the mix. Or artists or actors or dancers. When I talk to my friends and colleagues who write, we waste no time exposing our fears, our limitations, news of the first draft we threw in the trash and then rescued the next morning. We talk about quitting and giving up, and then we talk each other back to the desk, back to the words, back to the creative work.

With only a very few close and trusted friends can I talk about my sporadic desire to quit the mother game altogether—because of my own failings and the complicated needs of my children and my desire to concentrate on my writing. Only those indispensable few can pick me up off the floor and help me renew my commitment to the really hard work of raising my children, assuring me that the balance will be restored and we'll all live reasonably happy lives. With everyone else, especially with groups of other mothers, I still find myself smiling and nodding as I've been trained by my culture to do, and wading forward through the often-murky waters of life, wearing my happy mother guise.

To Contemplate

• Celebrate the good news by making a list of the ways that motherhood feeds and nourishes your creativity. If it's not a long list right now, don't worry. Pick one thing and write it down. Read it to yourself. Read it to your child. Marvel at the connection between your mothering and your creative work.

• In your present community (however you define it), do you feel you have a voice? Can you speak the truth about your experience of being a mother? Can you talk about your creative work? if not, it may be time to rethink your criteria for friendship and support. You deserve to feel known and valued for your true self.

Wise Words

"The more creative work I get to experience and get recognized for, the more I come home really interested in being a mother."
—Dee Paddock

"Maybe your kids will actually inspire you!"
—Moira Keefe

*"When I feel that tinge of resentment about them
(children), I realize it'll be over in all too short a
time. There's a sneaky little shift in there at
some point."*
—Christy Cutler

*"People say to me, 'Oh you're teaching kids—it
can't be very creative.' Believe it or not, it feeds my
creativity. I gain so much by playing with the kids.
My creativity takes marvelous spins and turns."*
—Gracie Carr

Chapter Four

The Invisibility Factor

"No one can make you feel inferior
without your consent."

—Anna Eleanor Roosevelt

(But they can try. And they will.)

—Coleen Hubbard

Even though we may be lucky enough to discover or enhance our creative work after becoming mothers, and even though we may survive the initial onslaught of children and eventually find our creative voice, we are apt to find ourselves silenced out in the larger world. Because our working culture doesn't seem to welcome mothers (even—or *especially*—in the arts), it may be necessary to downplay or even dismiss the fact that we are also raising children in order to maintain a presence in our creative field. And if, while raising children, we are passionately at work in our creative field, we sometimes feel we must "hide" this other part of ourselves to avoid being perceived as a less than desirable mother.

Some of the stories in this chapter about being "cast out"

and "made invisible" are not easy to read—a few are downright disturbing. In some cases, women pay dearly for the right to pursue their creative work *and* be a mother. But these stories are critical to share because they illustrate a common occurrence in the lives of creative mothers that I call The Invisibility Factor.

First we'll take a look at some women who feel they've had to diminish motherhood in order to be respected and taken seriously in their creative field. Then we'll follow the stories of women who feel pressure to hide their creative work in order to function within the bounds of traditional motherhood.

This story from my own life is a tale of lost innocence, about the time I first realized being a mother could be considered a liability in the larger world.

The "Baby List"

When I was in my mid-twenties, married for the first time and working at a large regional theatre, I had a meeting with my boss to discuss my job performance. I received a glowing report, a pat on the back, and a tiny raise. Thrilled at the recognition (this was my first "real" job in a field I loved), I turned to leave. Life was good! I was moving in the right direction and my path was unfolding before me. Then my boss cleared his throat and said pointedly, "Now, if we can just keep you off the baby list."

It took a second for me to realize the implied threat beneath his words—that if I were to become pregnant and have a child I could jeopardize my potential in the creative field I loved. I was stunned by the fact that this man, who I previously admired, would not only *think* such a thing, but *say it aloud to me at a job review!* I knew that my boss would never utter such a remark to a man, but it took years before I learned that these kinds of comments were considered professionally tasteless and completely off-limits during job interviews and performance reviews.

And, of course, I *did* add my name to the "baby list," giving birth to my first daughter a year and a half later—after continuing to rise in the organization and take on some singular responsibilities. But when I returned from my six-week maternity leave, I quickly realized that my beloved workplace, my creative home, was a decidedly child-*un*friendly place, and I was suddenly seen in a suspicious light by several high-ranking colleagues. The message from the top was that women with children couldn't participate in the priesthood of theatre, where those ordained on high worshipped only one God and had no false idols at home who needed their diapers changed, sometimes got sick unexpectedly, and altered one's presumed priorities.

I continued to work there under tense conditions, until my personal life fell into such chaos (a divorce, inadequate child care, a new relationship) that when I was "laid off" in a "departmental reorganization," I was devastated and relieved at the same time.

I had been cast out, with a big "M" for mother stamped on my forehead. I was deemed unworthy to stay where I once belonged. But at least I would no longer have to keep trying to hide the "messiness" of real life in a place where "life" was played out on carefully painted sets, and children made only the occasional guest appearance as audience members for holiday shows.

Jahnna Beecham, who faced similar obstacles in the world of regional theatre sums it up well:

> In the theatre, if you're a parent you're a pariah! Once you start having children, you realize it's impossible in the theatre.

Not surprisingly, Jahnna and a group of like-minded theatre people eventually created and managed The Gathering, a highly successful new play festival that ran for several years and welcomed playwrights, actors, and directors from across the country—*along with their children.*

I Don't Dress Like a Mom

In the previous chapter we met Dee Paddock, a therapist and national speaker whose creative work finds her on an airplane at least once a week, flying off to deliver a keynote address or facilitate a workshop on adoption. Because she is a woman in a mostly male field, and because she gets tired of responding to questions from busybodies about how "hard it must be to leave the children behind," she compensates by choosing a style of dress that helps her "hide" her motherhood and become visible in her creative work.

Most of the people I compete directly with in my field are men, some of whom have written two, three, four books already. I can't get my first book finished. Some of that is my own fault, but some of that is because I have so much pulling at me with three children that I haven't figured out how to sit down and get it written. Trying to travel and speak takes a lot of time, and I'm competing against men who have wives at home taking care of their kids.

When I'm traveling away from my family I'm very sensitive to the criticism about leaving my children. I emphasize that my kids are home with their father—that they're being "fathered." On the road, I try and minimize the mother part of me, to avoid that criticism. I wear pants, a black suit—like men do. I look nothing like a mom when I'm working.

Dee says this approach works well for her, but causes some confusion when she's back in her conservative suburban town. Once she's home, she suddenly finds herself making her work invisible to other moms.

> Then, when I'm at school with my kids, it's hard fitting in with the super-volunteer moms. I can't talk about my work with most people since very few people do what I do.

The result is that Dee feels invisible in both parts of her life, and only among family and friends can she "unveil" and give breath to her full identity. Still, she's quick to point out that despite the irritation of making her work or her motherhood "invisible" in certain situations, her life is unfolding in a positive, creative way. She feels fortunate to be paid well for her work, to be respected in her field, and to have a partner who fully participates in the care of their children.

For Aisha Zawadi, whom you're about to meet, a time of financial desperation brought the cloak of invisibility over her creative work *and* her sense of herself as a mother, in a particularly painful way.

Meet Aisha

Aisha Zawadi is an artist and teacher, and the single mother of a grade school–aged son. Before becoming a parent, she received her college degree in Fine Arts and focused on becoming a painter, working in acrylic abstract paintings. She fell easily into her local art scene, getting to know gallery owners and reaching the point where she had participated in a number of shows with fellow artist/friends.

> I was very involved in getting my pieces into shows—I was in three or four before Kahlil came along. Then, suddenly, everything changed. I'd been poor and struggling when it was just me and it didn't bother me. But to think of being a poor, struggling artist with a child—that was too much!

With no other means of support in sight, Aisha made the truly difficult decision to go on welfare—a decision that still causes her to visually shudder as she describes the experience.

> My family of origin always had enough money for us to eat, live in a good home, have nice clothes, be happy—we weren't rich, but we were living a middle-class life on an Air Force base. But once I had Kahlil, I had to go on welfare because my savings lasted only for his first five months, and my work as an artist couldn't support us. I wanted, more than anything to be with him. But welfare is a nasty, degrading system.

Because of Aisha's fierce love for her child, she not only became part of a system she loathed, but left her burgeoning art career behind. The invisible status of a mother on public assistance, coupled with the sudden loss of her creative work was a double blow.

> I feel that mothers should be with their children for as long as possible. Staying home with Kahlil was a necessity for me, but it was very hard. At least through welfare I got into my jewelry business, thanks to a program for women who

wanted to be entrepreneurs, where I learned how to manage a business and even got a small business loan to get started. That was a great opportunity—but it was horrible to be on welfare. I didn't want anyone to know. It's not a "feel good" system. Yet, actually, every person I met on welfare had more aspirations than the stereotype you hear about.

Aisha eventually went back to school to get her teacher's certificate, and created the middle school art program at an independent school where her son is also a student. After years of being the sole provider and parent, Aisha is relieved that Kahlil's father is now involved in helping to raise and support his son. With every other weekend free, Aisha is finding time to slowly return to painting.

But even though this story has a mostly happy ending, and Aisha keeps her outlook positive and loving, she carries the invisible scars of living through a woman's worst nightmare of invisibility. The loss of creative identity *and* financial support upon having a child creates a particularly demanding set of circumstances with very few options.

"Visible" Fathers

Women in all fields, at one time or another, have felt it necessary to hide or diminish their mother identity to avoid professional setbacks. We've all heard the moronic jokes about how the brains of new mothers turn to mush, and how, as a baby nurses at her mother's breast, a woman's brain cells flow out with the milk.

Why, then, does the opposite appear to be true for men? My husband reports that he was never once warned to stay off the "baby list"—not in New York publishing, not as a college professor, and not as the creative director for an Internet company. In fact, he feels that being a father is a professional asset, bringing with it an increased perception of respectability. Men with children are viewed as mature, responsible adults who become even more dedicated and loyal to their work once they have a "family to support." A recent blurb in *Newsweek* describing a study on this very subject began with the following provocative lead-in:

> Attention, Dads: don't let workplace worries keep you from your kid's soccer games. Men who make family a priority actually earn more than those who don't, says an upcoming study in the journal *Industrial Relations*.

Can you imagine how women's lives would be forever altered if the same were true for mothers?

But You Don't Really Work, Do You?

Sometimes women find that their creative work is invisible to other parents who either work a "real" job outside the home, or stay home full-time with their children. Creative work is rarely seen as "real" work with strict commitments and deadlines.

Jahnna Beecham recently had this experience at her children's school:

> There are parents who don't think I work, just because I write at home. I really hate saying "I have a deadline" every time I see someone from the school, in an attempt to justify why I can't drive on every fieldtrip, or go in every day and

assist in reading. Somebody said to me the other day, "You have no boss. You have no one who tells you that you have to work! Why can't you come in and volunteer?"

Mostly I don't discuss my writing with other people—either because it sounds show-offy, or because then they start saying, "I didn't call you because I didn't want to bother you and interfere with your artistic moment!"

The Donna Reed Piece

Because women's creative work is often seen by others as a "hobby" or as work that can easily be set aside in order to serve others, many women learn to be silent about their projects, and talk about their children, instead. Gracie Carr laments the difficulty of finding fellow mothers who can relate to her situation—she works full-time as a teacher during the day, and occasionally takes on a role in a local theatre production to feed her creative self.

Some stay-at-home moms can't understand why someone would want to—or have to—work in the first place. Then, doing a show that requires rehearsals at night—I don't even bother to bring that up.

But when asked if she feels she lives on the fringes of traditional motherhood because of her choices, Gracie takes a pause, smiles, and confesses:

I find some pleasure in that! Because the Donna Reed piece doesn't last long after the kids are about thirteen years old. The rope that holds them to us begins to fray, and then what do you have left?

If Gracie thwarts the Donna Reed image by teaching full-time and performing occasionally, then the woman you're about to meet just plain busts the stereotype to pieces.

Meet Clarice

Clarice Williams is an actress in her forties who currently lives and works in New York City, but it took her a long time to get there. For years, she and her former husband (who is also in the theatre) lived in various cities across the country, depending on their employment with regional theatres and universities. They also raised their young son, which wasn't easy given the long and arduous work schedules typical of most theatres. As their marriage unraveled, one of the sticking points for Clarice's husband was that theatre was "too important" to her. Clarice responds:

> Well, it IS important to me and I wasn't about to abandon
> it, especially given all the stress when the marriage ended.
> Also, I had nothing to fall back on, since acting was my
> only profession.

For a number of years, Clarice's son (we'll call him Jon) lived with her during the school year and spent summers with his dad. Clarice was living in a large East Coast city, where she could find acting work and Jon could be near relatives. Her former husband (we'll call him Ben) moved to another state to run a university theatre program, and eventually married. In their original custody arrangement, both parents had agreed that when Jon was older he would go to live with Ben during the school year and with Clarice for holidays and summers. So, when Jon moved to be with Ben, Clarice decided to pursue her longtime dream of living in New York:

> When Jon went back to be with his dad the house felt completely empty without him and I needed a real adventure. I had always wanted to live in New York and do theatre there, but knew it would be difficult with my son. Jon's dad lives in a suburban setting with a good school system and has a strong financial situation—and all of this gives a lot of stability to my son. But when I explain my situation to people, which I know is unique, they look at me with shock—like "How could you do such a thing?" It isn't easy, but the one thing I can say is that my son seems happy, which says a lot for a teenage boy. At a time when most kids smirk and say, "Yeah, right, okay Mom," he tells me twenty times a day that he loves me. Given the realities of the situation, I can't ask for anything more than that.

Though Clarice constantly calls on all of her creativity, flexibility and strength to arrange a life that provides stability and happiness for her son, and though Jon is clearly thriving, she often feels she is invisible in the ranks of traditional families. She fears being misunderstood as a mother who "abandoned" her son for her art, which couldn't be further from the truth. That would merely be an easy answer to a complicated equation and another example of our culture's stereotypical view that women can't manage these disparate roles. Clarice manages to raise her son with his father and stepmother, *and* pursue her work as an actress with grace, humor, and dedication. It just looks different on the outside and is therefore subject to unwarranted judgment.

Rated R

And finally, I offer you one last story that illustrates another taboo element of creativity that leads to invisibility. What happens when our creative work is rated R and not necessarily for the eyes and ears and sensibilities of our children? What's at risk for the mother who pens a steamy sex scene in her latest novel, or the mother who plays a drug-addicted prostitute in a little known play? Are you a "bad mother" if your creative work takes you to dark, unsavory, erotic, uncensored places meant for adults only? Will your children suffer the reputation of having a weird, disturbed mother who has no business stepping foot in the world of "regular" mom-dom?

Maria Katzenbach muses over this question in regard to her own work:

> Parenthood, and mothering in particular, can have an insidious influence on what you let yourself create. You know—you can't paint nude women. That would look bad! I started this huge collage six months ago and it's still sitting there. And I have this vision for it, but I'm not finishing it because Eve is naked and I have a son!
>
> Much of this feeling stems from our fear of emotionality, fear of the body, fear of the erotic, fear of life. I think that we live in a culture that's very afraid of these things, and the message is that a mother should not be alive in her womanhood. But so much of being an artist is an exploration of the feminine mysteries. It seems to me that mothers are expected to create in an infantile, cute way—like ducks. You're allowed to paint ducks, or hearts, but not nude women!

Rated "R" for Revealing

Sometimes we can form a kind of protective coating around our creative work by trying to coach others into understanding that the images we paint, the figures we sculpt in clay, the characters we play in a drama are not really us. These creations may ultimately reflect our souls and our psyches, but they are truly of our imagination. When I create a character in a play or book, that man or woman or child is a compilation of me, my family, my friends, strangers and all matter of free-floating influences from the universe. While these characters may carry aspects of me, *they are not me.*

But what happens when a woman's creative work is *truly* autobiographical? What's at risk for a mother who uses her creativity to tell a story about herself that is so raw, so honest, so deeply real that she sheds the cloak of invisibility forever, among strangers and friends—and her own children?

The Taboo Story

The first time I had the honor of watching Moira Keefe perform was in a comic piece about surviving first-time motherhood. Using a watermelon tucked in her overalls to first represent the audacious size of full-term pregnancy, and later to represent the baby herself, Moira kept the audience in a fit of sustained laughter all evening.

In another of her shows, *Life Before the Crisis*, Moira is facing forty and a mid-life crisis, and she realizes everyone around her is taking Prozac. For the entire piece, she rides a bicycle around the stage in a visual representation of lost freedom and youth. But with her characteristic touch, Moira turns the bicycle upside down for a scene about enduring her very first mammogram—the female right of passage into true mid-life. Squeezing her breast between the spokes of the wheel, she simulates the degrading and uncomfortable process of having one's breast squeezed, lifted, and pressed flat for the series of x-rays.

Needless to say, the female portion of the audience howled with laughter at the truth behind Moira's exaggerated antics. In just a few seconds she managed to capture and convey both the absurdity and poignancy of an aspect of women's lives that is rarely discussed in public. And I'm sure that many men go home after seeing her show and say to the women they love, "Is that what it's really like? I had no idea!"

But telling the truth about pregnancy and childbirth and mid-life angst can't hold a candle to the subject of Moira's newest piece, *The Crisis: There's a Rat in My Three-Car Garage*. When Moira and her family left the Rocky Mountains for suburban San Diego, to allow her husband to pursue a professorship at UCSD, she left behind a tight community of friends and an artistic home. She suffered the usual feelings of dislocation and upheaval, brought about by the unfamiliar beach culture of California and her look-alike suburban development where she claims she can hear the toilets flush next door.

To make matters worse, she says, "We paid a quarter of a million dollars for our house and there's a rat living in our garage!" But the rat wasn't the real crisis; the true crisis came when she found she was unexpectedly pregnant, and unprepared to raise a third child. Moira's husband strongly believed that their family was already complete, and Moira feared she would lose her creative identity completely with another child to raise. After a wrenching decision to end the pregnancy, Moira fell into a depression that lasted for several years. While everyone thought she was doing fine, Moira struggled to get through each day—

excruciatingly aware that she was living with her own invisible rat.

Finally, Moira ended her silence and began opening up to friends. To her surprise, she encountered support and encouragement—and other stories about mothers in happy marriages choosing to end a pregnancy. She decided to explore the taboo subject through performance, and completed her most provocative theatre piece to date. Listen to what Moira has to say, looking back on her decision:

I think because I had two kids and never had a full-time nanny, it's been hard to get launched, professionally. My piece addresses the terrible struggle of deciding to go through an abortion. I felt if I had one more child, that was the end of me creatively. I mean, how much can one person give? My regret was really strong there for many years, though in my gut, I believe it was the right thing to do. But it took its toll. I think if it was a man having to decide about work and children, it wouldn't be so hard. On a daily basis I struggle with how much I can give my husband, my two kids, and friendships I want to nurture. How do you do that and still have time for yourself?

When I did a first reading of *The Crisis*, fifteen women from my community showed up. I was really nervous. But some of the women I thought would freak out were really understanding. Sometimes I do this piece back-to-back with my bicycle piece, and people seem to respond to the juxtaposition—that first I can be this wise-ass talking about Prozac, and then I can go on to talk about these other, deeper issues.

Like Dee Paddock who had to endure losing her child before finding her creative gifts, Moira had to endure the guilt and sadness following her abortion before finding the seeds for her important new work. Because she is courageous enough to risk being visible, Moira will ultimately help to free other women from the "taboo" status of their similar stories.

I love what Harriet Lerner says about this in her book, *The Mother Dance*:

> Most mothers are not in touch with all that they are capable of feeling, because when impulses and sentiments are culturally taboo, the power of repression and denial is great.

My hat goes off to all the mothers in this book (and out in the world) who are brave enough to fight off invisibility and share their gifts of expression. One by one, through their creativity, and through their character and stamina, they are pushing the parameters of traditional motherhood to open up some new, and stunning territory for the mothers of the next generation—our daughters.

To Contemplate

• Think about your own experiences of being invisible, both as a mother and in your creative work. Is the "invisibility" imposed on you by outside forces, or is it self-imposed? Are there ways you can risk "showing up" today—even for a few moments?

• Have you lived through an experience as a mother that has left invisible scars? (It needn't be something as dramatic as losing a child, going on welfare, or having an abortion.) Are there aspects of that experience that might be healed through your creative work? Can you reach out to other mothers who've had a similar experience and end your isolation?

Wise Words

Sometimes we make our motherhood invisible in order to establish, or maintain work out in the world. Sometimes we make our creative work invisible in order to join the ranks of other mothers. Sometimes we keep our work hidden from our children, in the fear that our subject matter will reflect poorly on our ability to be good mothers. Sometimes we make life choices that we think better serve our children or their school community, or our bosses or partners—putting our creative work aside. We stop before we've finished, convincing ourselves that perhaps it's best, after all, to just be . . . well, *invisible*.

But before you give in to those voices telling you it's all too hard, take solace from these words:

> *"Everything changes. Don't assume it will never change. Don't be so worried about working all the time. Better ideas can come through simplicity. Don't be too practical, or try to find out too much ahead of time. If I'd known I wouldn't have produced much art over these last ten years, I'd have never had children. And that would have been really sad, because with the strength and ideas and philosophy I have in me now, I'm about to do the best work of my life."*
> —Lady McCrady

> *"Creativity is a deep-seated experience in your soul. A baby can't take it from you. It may be quiet for a*

little while and you may have to listen to your baby's cry instead of your inner yearnings, but you're in control of this. Your child will feed off of your creativity, because when you're creating you're a happier person. So don't think, 'It'll never come back.' Because it will always be in your heart, your head, in your soul, and no child can suck that out of you. Don't let that happen!"
—Gracie Carr

"Take the long view. Ask employers for what you need (they often give it to you). Who you are and what you do can enrich your whole family. I remember thinking that my dad loved what he did, and that he chose education over business, which is what his father expected him to do. When I was facing a very difficult time, moaning about how theatre and my love for it had seemed to cause so many problems in my marriage, my dad said, 'But it's the only thing you ever wanted to do since you were small. It's who you are.' That reminder went a long way."
—Clarice Williams

"When you get down, it's sometimes hard to pull yourself up. But I always go to the opposite of that feeling, which is love. Whenever I'm feeling really bad, I know I'll come back to love."
—Aisha Zawadi

Chapter Five

Your Creativity Cycle, Your Children's Life Cycle

*"We need to recognize
that there will inevitably be some stages
and
seasons in our child's life that, at best,
we'll just muddle through."*

—Harriet Lerner, Ph.D.
The Mother Dance

It's September—the most difficult month of the year for you. Something about the falling leaves and change of light makes you feel sad, and virtually unable to have a creative thought. Besides, your daughter is starting high school and every time you look at her almost grown-up face you want to cry.

Or maybe it's summer—your favorite time of the year. All you want to do is take your third grader and his friends to the pool and watch them perfect their dives. You feel a little guilty about not working, but you know that soaking in the sunshine is a way to restore your soul.

Or maybe it's almost your birthday and the thought of turning forty has you looking at your life like never before. Suddenly you want to try a completely new creative venture. But the teacher at your child's preschool has you convinced they can't do finger painting without your expertise and they need you to be there every morning next week.

You've almost finished a monumentally important project—thanks to months of heroic creative effort on your part. All you want is to be left alone so you can complete it, but your son and daughter are suddenly fighting all the time and more needy than ever before. You feel literally pulled apart.

Do any of these scenarios sound familiar? Every woman involved in creative work understands that we move through cycles of creativity, depending on the hour of the day, the day of the week, the season of the year, the particular decade of our life, and where we are in the scope of a specific creative undertaking. And, of course, as mothers we cycle in and out of various seasons of parenting, depending on the ages of our children, our own biological age, and the dance of attachment and separation that accompanies each stage of being a parent.

Add to this the various, ongoing cycles, both predictable and utterly astounding, that our children spin through before our very eyes, and we're suddenly dealing with the mathematical equivalent of "cycle squared." No wonder we sometimes feel as if we're riding one of those high-tech roller coasters designed to take us careening through loops inside of loops, sometimes hanging upside down and no longer sure that gravity is a given fact.

As mothers involved in creative work, we are perhaps especially vulnerable to the effects of these intertwined cycles of age and stage, of time and place. In this chapter, we'll explore a variety of internal and external cycles, and what's possible and problematic during each. Let's begin by looking at what may happen to a woman's creativity during her child's infancy, toddler years, preschool years, young childhood and adolescence, teen years . . . and beyond.

Baby, Oh, Baby

Some women report that they experienced a powerfully creative period during pregnancy, especially in the case of a first child when there weren't others at home who needed care. This *can* be a wonderful time to dive into creative work, turning the steady blast of maternal heat toward an unfinished project, or something as new and unknown as the child growing inside. Other women report that pregnancy was a time of nesting, napping, dreaming, and chose to float with their inner rhythms rather than concentrate on creative work. Most of us recall our dream life during pregnancy as particularly vivid and creative, enhancing and sharpening our intuition and our senses.

But no matter our individual experience, almost all of us feel completely unprepared for what happens to our creative work upon the actual arrival of a baby. Our own schedules go out the window as we struggle to learn a new and complicated schedule of feeding, holding, bathing, diapering, and trying to find odd pockets of time for sleep and rest. Where once we were free to ponder and tinker and follow our inner creative voice, now we are on call twenty-four hours a day to the strong and outward cries of a needy newborn.

Then, after a month or so of absolute chaos, something strange begins to happen to some of us. We wander to our office or studio or corner of the dining room, focus our bleary eyes on a scrap, a scrawl, a page of music, a grant application and decide then and there that we're getting back to our work. It almost becomes a challenge of Olympic proportion: *I will do this again, no matter the crying baby, the leaking breasts, the unspeakable fatigue! I can do it all, and I'm starting today!*

I have a picture that my husband took of me when my middle child was around that one-month age. I'm sitting in front of my computer with tiny Natalie strapped to my chest in a cloth carrier. Her dark hair is visible above the opening of the denim sack, and my own hair is wild from not having had a shower yet that day. I remember that I was trying to finish a play, and I can still recall the frenzy with which I approached the work—stemming from a combination of adrenaline, sleep deprivation, and fierce determination not to completely lose myself again.

Despite the photograph, in reality I did very little work when Natalie was an infant. She had severe colic for her first three months and needed to be held and walked and rocked almost every moment of her waking life. Still, I occasionally wandered zombielike to my desk and penned a line or two of dialogue, and it was vitally important to me at the time! No one could have made me believe then that being still and patient through The Time of Great Colic wouldn't cost me my creative self.

With the wisdom of age, I now look back and realize that I could have used those few unchained hours to rest, read, take a walk, or for heaven's sake take a shower. I might have emerged more replenished and engaged. I didn't know then that a time of quietness in my creative life was a useful and necessary thing and would be followed, eventually, by a time of renewed energy and productivity.

Big Bursts and Tiny Bursts

The experience of creativity during the newborn phase is different for each of us, and has much to do with all the variables: whether we have to return to a wage job soon after birth, whether we have help or not, whether our babies are easy or fussy, whether we had difficult births or textbook deliveries.

Gracie Carr remembers:

I enjoyed a big burst of writing and composing songs when my daughter was a little baby. It was compulsive—you know, "I can do this. I can be a mother and still hear people perform my songs." I was very productive, but I wasn't taking care of myself in other ways. And yet, it worked at the time. It fit my life. I could compose at home with her.

Moira Keefe remembers having a completely different experience with each of her two daughters:

When my first was a baby I did nothing but throw Mom and Margarita parties (you bring your baby, I'll make the margaritas). I didn't write until she was two. But Rocky, my second, was an easy baby and I knew what I was in for. I was pretty productive until she was a year. I produced a women's theatre festival and wrote a play. How the hell did I do that?!

And while both Gracie and Moira experienced the "big burst" of creativity, Maria Katzenbach remembers that the "tiny burst" approach worked best for her when her son was born:

When children are really young, their lives are so intertwined with yours that you just have to let your creativity "be" in that relationship. Pour it all out to them when they're really young, and if you have to take your creativity out into the world, if you just HAVE to, make it very intense and very tiny. It's a burst, and that's it. Don't try to do anything for sustained periods. Accept that this is just for now.

The Stroller Years

After raising three toddlers and being closely associated with dozens more, I've come to call the years between one and three The Stroller Years. This period of time in parents' lives becomes a repetitive drill of trying to transport and restrain children who aren't predictably mobile, yet eager to be out in the world. We spend countless hours folding up the stroller, putting it in the car, taking it out of the car, unfolding it again, and arranging our toddler and all her gear in the seat and attached basket. We jam strollers through unaccommodating doors; we manipulate them on elevators and escalators, and develop an uncanny knack for finding the ramp access to any building. We can hold a squirming child, purse, and diaper bag in one hand while using the other hand and a spare foot to unlatch the gear that releases the folded stroller like a toy clown in a box.

During The Stroller Years, the world actually seems to revolve around this single piece of equipment, this miniature hammock on wheels. I recently caught super model Cindy Crawford on a morning news show, discussing strollers with a magazine editor. The two mothers raved on and on about a specific, seven-pound designer travel stroller and even took turns folding and unfolding it for the television audience!

The madness behind the stroller fixation really just confirms the undisputed fact that life with toddlers is a mixed blessing: they're funny and cute, *but you have to watch them every single minute.* Because they are mobile, they are always an inch away from nine hundred kinds of danger. And all that vigilance and worry and running around and counting heads is exhausting. It leaves you with very few brain cells available for creative work, and can make you miss the immobile, sleepy, infant months.

The specific day in my life when I realized that I was captive in the crazy land of The Stroller Years is still etched in my memory. I had taken an out-of-town friend (whose only child was grown) for a drive in the mountains, with my newborn and toddler strapped in their car seats. Thankfully, both girls slept for a good hour, giving the adults some uninterrupted time for conversation—something I desperately needed! We talked about my chaotic life, and how I hadn't been able to spend much time writing, and my friend reminded me how soon that would all change as the girls grew up and became more independent. (This advice, as you know, makes sense only in hindsight and is usually of little help at the time!)

When we arrived at the charming resort where we planned to have lunch and a walk around the lake, I was feeling confident that I was in control of the outing, for once. The fact that I had two very needy little ones with me and that I was painfully exhausted wouldn't spoil our lovely afternoon.

I opened the back of my car and pulled out the heavy and cumbersome "double stroller" for our walk. I set the contraption on the pavement and closed the trunk. Then I reached down to unhook the latch—but suddenly, and inexplicably, couldn't remember how to open the stroller. This was something I'd been doing daily for months and years. I stared at the stroller like it was a foreign object, certain that I was having a stroke or some other kind of medical emergency.

This momentary amnesia was truly frightening; I had a flash of what it must be like to actually have a disease like Alzheimer's. The longer I stared at the stroller, the more stupid and numb I felt. Finally, my friend came over and asked if she could help. I didn't even have the words to explain what was happening to me, so I just smiled and told her that the dumb stroller wasn't cooperating. By then, my daughters were beginning to squirm and protest in their car seats and sweat dripped from my forehead. By some sheer piece of good luck, I finally found the latch and the stroller unfolded into its double capacity, sedan-length glory.

I don't remember much else about that day, except for a nagging worry that something was truly wrong with me—that I had, for instance, a horrible brain tumor that was eating away at my memory. Why else would I have forgotten how to open a stroller? Would I suddenly forget how to drive the car on the way home?

Later that evening, I shared the incident with my husband, thinking he would be as scared and concerned as I was and insist that I go to the hospital at once for a CAT scan and write out my will. Instead, he laughed. *Laughed!* And then he managed to reassure me that the whole thing was no big deal, that out of exhaustion and maternal overload I'd experienced a momentary and ordinary lapse in my short-term memory. He equated it with suddenly forgetting the name of a good friend or favorite restaurant, or misplacing a set of keys.

Eventually, I was able to laugh about that day, and I realized it explained my complete inability to concentrate on creative work. My head was filled with stroller latches and car seats and cracker crumbs and snatches of tunes from *Sesame Street*, creating a temporary lack of room on the hard drive for creative thought and impulse.

The point of this story is to let yourself off the hook if you're busy with a baby or toddler and you're not accomplishing all that you'd like to in your creative work. If there's one lesson I've learned along the way, it's this: *You can do it all and have it all—don't let anyone tell you differently. But it's not possible to do it all and have it all, ALL of the time.*

I love a particular story that Anne Lamott (one of my true mother/writer heroes!) shares in her book *Operating Instructions: A Journal of My Son's First Year*, in which she writes hilarious and poignant entries about being a new mother. Totally immersed in the work and joy of her son, Anne loses touch with her writer self—even when she realizes that her new book is about to be released and has garnered high praise from every corner:

> So that's all good news. I really can't relate, though. I keep thinking, Well that's nice. I'm pleased and it's a huge shot in the arm—still, I keep thinking that the jig is just about up. The phone will ring and the authorities will at first gently try to get me to confess that I didn't acutally write the book, and if I continue to claim that I did, they'll turn vicious, abusive: "Look at yourself! You're a goddamn mess. You've got a functioning IQ of less than 100, your nerves are shot, your hands tremble, you're covered with milk and spit-up. You have trouble writing out checks, yet you want us to believe you produced a novel? Well. We don't think so." Then they'll make me go get a job with the phone company.

This feeling of being cut off from our creative self, of feeling like a "fraud" because we're not focusing intensely on our creative endeavors, is a feeling that plagues most of us when our children are small. We think, somehow, that we should be able to overcome the day-to-day demands on our time and our psyche and still feel passionately connected to our creative life.

The woman you're about to meet is currently in the red hot center of this specific cycle.

Meet Wendi

Wendi Schneider is an artist and photographer who was immersed in a successful creative career before marrying and giving birth to her son, Leo. She combines a sweet Southern charm (she's originally from Memphis) with a captivating hipness garnered from her years of living and working in the New York art world. With her hair swept back in an easy up-do and wearing trendy black overalls, she looks too put together to be the frazzled mother of a three-year-old that she readily admits to being.

Her experience of motherhood comes with the given circumstance that she's older than many of the mothers in her son's preschool class.

> Most of them are in their 20's or early 30's, and I'm 44. They're really nice, and I've befriended them, even though we're at different stages in our lives. Although we're not friends through creative endeavors, we bond over motherhood.

Sharing her creative self with the preschool moms hasn't been a significant problem for Wendi. Since her home is filled with her paintings, photographs, and the antiques she now sells online, Wendi's creativity is hanging on the walls, so to speak. "I try," she says, "to have people over so they can see what I do, both the kids and the moms. I figure if I have them over, they can get a better sense of who I am in addition to a mother."

The challenge for Wendi at the moment is feeling that she's left her creative identity behind, because she's taken a break from photography and painting to focus on her son and her burgeoning antiques business. Though anyone with a three-year-old understands the temporary shift of focus, Wendi feels creatively blocked and distanced from her previous work.

It's different now. I have a husband and a child and it just feels like such a dramatic change in my life. I'm sure it has something to do with Leo being three. It's very draining at times. I was on my own until I was 40 and did what I wanted. Worked for myself, worked when I wanted to—that worked well for me.

The day I interviewed Wendi, she'd survived one of those mornings-from-hell that make every mother doubt her sanity and stamina:

I woke up early because I was going to try to get some things done before Leo and Eddie got up. And we had a houseguest who was leaving, and he said he'd go get some coffee and bagels. So he left and I was trying to work, and then Leo woke up. Then our friend came back and said he'd fix Leo breakfast, only Leo didn't want a bagel. He was shrieking and crying and he didn't want to get dressed and he wanted French toast strips for breakfast, and we had about ten minutes before we needed to leave for preschool. So I told him, "Okay, you can either put your shoes and socks on or go upstairs for a timeout." Then his dad finally got him into his shoes and socks and made him the French toast strips. And, in the meantime, I was trying to return a phone call to arrange a playdate for Leo and get some antique fabric packed in a box to be shipped off and I knocked my coffee all over the desk—on the bills, on the photographs, on the fabric. By then it was nine o'clock and Leo's covered in syrup and we were supposed to be at school. The sink was full of dirty dishes and our friend was leaving, and I didn't even get to say goodbye. It was just one of those days.

What feels like blocked creativity to Wendi looks to the rest of us like absolute fatigue, and the natural consequences of life with a small child. But once again, if we're isolated as a mother and then isolated from our creative work because we're utterly busy being a mother, is it any wonder that our sense of self takes a pounding?

By the way, just to reinforce that Wendi hasn't lost her creativity, notice the photographs that illustrate this book. They are Wendi's work.

Gone All Day!

I derive great pleasure from telling Wendi (and all my friends with small children still at home) about the great reward that lies ahead for her—drum roll, please!—*full day kindergarten*! In less than two years, Leo will attend school five days a week for six solid hours, and Wendi will begin to recapture huge chunks of her creative life. She won't even believe, until she experiences it herself, the fresh opportunities that arise when a child goes off to school.

There *is* something provident in the set-up of our educational system: just when we reach near burnout from years of intense parenting and just when our children are ready for new horizons, the kindergarten door opens and parent and child begin life anew. My own mother says she can still vividly recall the day her youngest (my brother Dan) went to kindergarten. She tells me that after she signed him in and stayed to make sure he was doing fine, she drove home and took a long, solitary bath—the first she'd had in nine years—to celebrate the successful launch of three children into the world.

When *my* youngest went to kindergarten, I stood in the back of the room for fifteen minutes and watched her make friends with a little boy at the water table, filling and emptying cup after cup of bright blue water. She barely looked up when I said good-bye, so eager was she to finally attend school like her sisters and be a "big girl." I strolled over to the principal's office where some staff members were hosting a coffee for parents of kindergart-ners—mostly as a kind of "safe" zone for those moms and dads leaving their first or only five-year-olds. I poured myself a cup of coffee and looked around at all the nervous parents, trying to remember what it felt like to leave my oldest daughter on her first day of school six years before.

Suddenly I felt a few tears well up, and as I wiped them away, another mother turned to me and said, "I know just how you feel. I didn't think I'd be this sad, but I've been crying all morn-ing."

I started to respond, but then bit my lip and kept silent. I didn't think she was ready to hear the truth—that I was crying tears of *happiness*! That I was overjoyed at the thought of going back home to a quiet house where, while I probably would forgo the bath my mother still remembers, I would spend the morning writing without distraction. My daughter now had a roomful of new friends and bright blue water to play with, and I had hours ahead with which to begin to become myself, once again.

Part-Time Taxi Driver

As rejuvenating and creatively productive as the school years can be, they contain a few pitfalls that you should be prepared for. Just when you get used to the astonishing fact that a portion of every weekday is yours alone to spend on your own work, a creeping sense of those delicious six hours going by all too fast may set in and make you long for more. You feel a bit guilty thinking this (after all, good mothers miss their children all day and count the minutes until they return!), but the luxury of getting lost in your work is compromised by having to make an abrupt return trip to the "mainly mother" identity. No sooner have you dropped your children off at school when it's time to turn around again and retrieve them.

Also be warned that endless volunteer tasks at your child's school can eat huge portions of your time if you allow it to happen. This is a trap I'm particularly vulnerable to (remember the story I told on myself at the beginning of this book?), as are many mothers who do their creative work at home. How do you say no to an understaffed school trying to nurture our children with a miniscule budget and little support, especially when it looks to the world like you're just at home "playing"? Be prepared to choose a select number of volunteer activities and practice saying no in a kind but steady voice.

Listen to how Moira Keefe describes the strange disappearance of the six precious hours when her kids are at school and she's supposed to be writing and marketing her performances:

I used to think that toddlerhood was the worst—especially if you didn't have any help. But now, in a strange way, I think that older kids are tougher. You have those six hours when they're in school, but that's all you have! By the time you get them out the door and clean up after breakfast, someone calls from school and needs you to drive for a field trip. Then you have to pick them up an hour early for the dentist; then they have volleyball practice. I always feel like I'm running and running.

That frantic pace grows in intensity as children get older and the pressure to introduce enriching activities into their already full lives emerges. This might include team sports, music or dance lessons, art class, martial arts, swimming, gymnastics—the list goes on and on. And it's all well and good for the development of our offspring, but it necessarily involves a parent (or hired sitter) spending many after-school hours as a part-time taxi driver, remembering to bring along the soccer shoes, the ballet tights, the juice, the snack, the permission slip, and supplies to entertain younger children (or ourselves) during the long and often boring wait for a lesson to end.

Suddenly, a halfway successful day spent deep in creative work turns into high-speed, high anxiety. The gas tank is always on empty, our children seem tired and cranky, and our own reserves of energy and patience become strained. Where once our children followed *our* schedule, we now become slaves to their overbooked kiddy calendars.

But it's wise to remember that *we* bear direct responsibility for creating this kind of loony after-school schedule. It may be helpful to examine whether or not our own vicarious needs, rather than our children's, are fueling the incessant quest for more and better classes, teams, and "enriching" experiences.

In their book *Hyper-Parenting: Are You Hurting Your Child by Trying Too Hard*, authors Alvin Rosenfeld M.D. and Nicole Wise offer a balancing perspective:

> As the temptation to hyper-parent increases, so do the opportunities. In the school-age years—which typically start by a child's third birthday nowadays, if not sooner—parents feel they should immerse themselves in the details of children's academic, athletic, and social lives. All that, as they continue intensive efforts to enrich their child's free time with experiences to enhance their development.
>
> What really should be beginning to happen as children get older is that they start to take over more responsibility for their own lives, and their parents start to let go.

This is excellent advice, though sometimes torturous to follow. "Letting go" is perhaps the most difficult part of being a parent, and it happens in tiny, daily, barely discernable increments. But if we're to make the transition to the next cycle, that of mothering our teenagers, it's vitally important that the process begins during the taxi driver years.

One Foot Out the Door

As my oldest daughter closes in on her most highly anticipated watermark on the path to freedom—learning to drive—I realize I've survived three years of being the mother of a teen. And I've developed a couple of theories about how this particular cycle affects my creative work.

First of all, on a purely physical level, I think something weird is going on. As Allie grows more beautiful every day, more interesting, more full of grace, I find myself in a physical decline marked by gray hair, laugh lines, gravity-impaired flesh, and the advent of bifocals (that vision thing again—I now need a *double* lens with which to make sense of my world!).

If you have a teenager you've surely noticed this, and I'm concerned that no one in the science fiction world is concerned. I mean, it seems obvious that through some kind of invisible umbilical cord, my energy, youth and vitality are being siphoned away and pumped into my blossoming daughter. Her moon is full and radiant, while mine wanes and disappears behind milky clouds. It may be that aliens are conducting massive experiments on human maturation, using my daughter and me as their unknowing guinea pigs, and frankly, I want it to stop!

This poignant awareness of the gap between youth and middle age seems to be an unavoidable byproduct of mothering teens. So is the indisputable fact that very soon these student drivers and near graduates will go off and leave us to lead independent lives. The creativity cycle during these years feels tied to a sense of both impending loss *and* freedom, and to the potency of our individual mid-life issues.

As our teens practice separation on a daily basis, we too begin to rehearse for a time in our life when the dilemma of mothering and creating is no longer applicable to our lives. Already, the sheer volume of time spent physically mothering my daughter is greatly diminished. Let's face it—she's not home all that often. She self-monitors her study and social needs. She does her own laundry and can make herself a simple meal, if needed. She makes lists for herself of things she wants to accomplish, and has dreams and plans independent of her family.

This isn't to say, however, that she doesn't *need* me. In fact, on a psychological level, she needs me more than ever and we spend a huge amount of time talking through weighty issues:

driving, dating, school pressures, world events, college applications, friends, the Internet, fashion, the female body—you get the idea. Because this ongoing dialogue is so important and intense, and because I must necessarily worry more now that my daughter is out in the world, I have come to feel that the mothering of a teen is some of the most difficult work in the entire cycle.

As Dee Paddock explains:

I'm the most productive now that my kids are more independent as teenagers. And I like them more now—I'm more inclined to want to spend time with them. I think that if my husband and I lose focus and screw up during our children's teenage years, it's what we'll most regret.

The Empty Nest

Beyond the teen years is that almost unimaginable time in a mother's life called "the empty nest." I wanted desperately to interview a mother with grown children who would tell me that once the children have been launched into the world, the worry and angst and self-doubt just magically disappear. I wanted to meet a woman who eased through that ultimate developmental cycle and then just as magically refocused all of her energy and time back on her creative career. I wanted to somehow be assured that at that point in time, we just move forward in our age, experience, and wisdom—without looking back on our several decades as a mother.

Well, I didn't meet that woman. And I'm not sure she exists. But I did meet a vibrant, interesting, candid woman named Mary Flower, who gave me a perspective I wasn't expecting.

Meet Mary

Mary Flower was born into a family of musicians. As one of six children, she has early memories of sitting around the table singing, and of the family music room, which featured two pianos so that her older sisters could play duets. But Mary was the only family member to pursue a professional career in music, becoming a blues guitarist and singer with an impressive performance résumé.

> I've played guitar and been a singer since I was eleven years old. I'm fifty-one now, and music is all I've ever really known how to do. I've taught since I was a teenager, recorded three CD's and a vinyl album years ago, and appeared on a number of other CD's. I do concerts and tour around the country teaching workshops. I'll do seven workshops this summer—where adults go to rekindle the passion they once had and to immerse themselves in music with some master musicians from around the world.

As you can see, Mary's career is flourishing during this period in her life when her son and daughter, who are in their early twenties, are off living independent lives. But it wasn't always the case. After her babies were born, Mary stopped touring and focused her energies on raising her children and trying to remain a visible presence in the local folk music scene.

She admits that it was difficult to keep a balance in her life, since her performance schedule kept her out late at night, and then she would have to get up very early with her children. And she says that she lost a lot of confidence in herself during those years because she never had as much time as she knew she needed to feel practiced and polished before a performance. But what haunts her most of all is the sense that she didn't focus enough attention on her children during those early years.

> I guess I have regrets, looking back. I don't think I knew how to be a mom. I don't think anyone does. I didn't read a lot of books on how to be a mom. I just look back with regret that when they were very young I tried to work part-time when childcare options weren't the best. And when your children are small, you need to be with them. That's my advice to the world. Be there, until it's time for them to go to school.
>
> I always feared that while I was waiting for my children to grow up, the world would pass me by and I'd forget how to master my art. You want to jump back in—but you just can't jump too soon. I just wish someone had said to me, "This is the most important job you'll ever have in your life."

It's so interesting to me how long the guilt and second-guessing of our parenting choices stay with us. Though Mary's children are doing well, and tell her that they truly appreciate the sacrifices she made for them when she stopped touring, she still chides herself for long-ago decisions. Though she gave the world a gift each time she took her abundant talents and shared them with an audience, she still lingers on the regrets of the past.

Mary isn't alone in this—I've had many a grandmother tell me that you never, never stop wondering and worrying about your children. Like Mary, perhaps we're just destined to sing the mother blues, and genetically wired to feel regret as we look back.

But we must also go easy on ourselves as we move through the cycles of mothering and doing our creative work. None of it is particularly easy, and hindsight isn't always particularly accurate. So take heart in Mary's final words: "I did as well as I could do at the time. That's what I have to keep remembering."

Seasonal Cycles

Regardless of the specific age of your child, there may be certain times during the calendar year that are more problematic for your creative work. The women I interviewed identified some common seasonal obstacles to creativity including back to school, the winter holidays, spring fever, and summer vacation.

September is always a heightened time as children and parents make the transition from the flexibility of summer to the fixed schedules of the school year. You may find yourself ready to make a new, creative start as your children begin a new school term, and yet, many of us find those first few months filled with a flurry of demands on our time and our psyche. First, there's the endless gathering of sports physicals and immunization records, signing enrollment and emergency cards, paying for books and activities, arranging carpools and after-school care, meeting teachers, attending back-to-school nights, and figuring out how much time you can afford to give to various volunteer committees.

Then there are the hours spent processing with your child how the new year is progressing, how the social scene is playing out, how to get back in the groove of homework, or how to deal with a not-so-favorite subject or teacher. By the time the kids are in sync and things feel smoothed out, you may find yourself mentally exhausted and distanced from your work.

My solution to the fall malaise is to take a cue from my children and engage in some rituals that mark the beginning of a new year (let's face it—even as adults we fall back on the old school calendar to order our year). I buy my own version of "school supplies"—new pens and pencils and journals. I clean off my desk, fill in my daybook, and make lists of things I want to accomplish. Though I stop short of buying a backpack or one of those sweaters embroidered with apples and autumn leaves, I definitely find ways to remind myself that I, too, am beginning a new term in my creative work.

And right when everyone has found her rhythm, December approaches with its various cultural holidays. Despite a yearly vow not to be buried by holiday madness, I always find it challenging to accomplish much of anything during December. We could go on and on about how women get trapped into being the CEO's of holidays, but that's a different book. Suffice it to say, that for me at least, I've lived through enough Decembers to know that the best I can do is simply hunker down in the cold and dark of winter and wait for a bit of creative thaw on January 1st.

The official beginning of a new year is an obvious time to regroup, rethink, and recommit to your creative work. The kids go back to school after several weeks at home, the holidays are over, and January and February spread before us like vast, uncharted continents. This is prime time for increased energy and concentration, with little to distract us other than the newspaper ads for beach vacations and cruises.

And then comes spring, with its milder weather and promise of gardens full of lush, gorgeous flowers. Many women report that the March to May sector leaves them too restless to stay indoors and focus on creative work. They suddenly want to leave the warmth of their office or studio and head outside to rake out flowerbeds and remove storm windows. I usually *think* about partaking in these lusty chores, but then take myself for a stroll around the Botanic Gardens instead, relishing someone else's handiwork with tulips and crocus. I think the antidote to spring fever is to simply give in (at least part of the time) and know that reconnecting with the natural world feeds our winter-weary creative souls.

And once you've done that, you'd better fasten your seat belt, get out the camp brochures, and get ready for the white-knuckled ride we call summer. Almost every one of the women I interviewed voted summer as the most difficult time to accomplish their creative work. And the number one reason is—you guessed it!—*the children are home for at least ten weeks!* Suddenly, your days to yourself are gone. Vanished. And you're left with confusing and expensive decisions about classes, camps, babysitters, and family vacations. Forget trying to work if there is even the possibility of a family vacation looming. Jahnna Beecham describes beautifully what happens when you try to plan a family vacation and deadlines for a creative project at the same time:

> Here's what always happens. You schedule a vacation for April, say, because your book is due in mid-March. Well, April rolls around and we're in Boston and we're having to do this last minute rewrite on a big book project. So I'm sitting at the desk in our hotel room trying to finish the last paragraph and the kids are standing at the door waiting for me, screaming at me to finish so we can go ride the swan boats. It got so bad that I finally made everyone go stand in the bathroom—Malcolm and the two kids—until I could finish the last few sentences!

I don't have any brilliant suggestions for the summer dilemma. I've tried everything, and the best I've come up with is a schedule that asks me to get up at sunrise, crank up the air conditioner in my office, work until the sun passes my window and the kids get up, then pack a marginally nutritious lunch and hang out with my kids at the local pool for the bulk of the afternoon. I may not write a best-seller on this schedule, but at the end of August I don't feel regret that I missed those long, lazy afternoons of damp magazines, sunblock, chlorine-tinted hair, and the sight of my sleek, brown daughters playing like dolphins in the water.

I'm drawn to the absolute truth within the sparse words by Harriet Lerner that I quoted at the beginning of this chapter. Through some of our children's cycles, we can only "muddle" through, improvise, and tap the tiniest reserves of our creativity. We can only do what's possible, given the ages of our children, our own cycles of creativity, and the seasons of the year. But we must keep in mind that by "muddling" on a daily, weekly, yearly basis, we *can* accumulate a substantial body of our creative work. And while we're "muddling," we're watching our children grow up and sometimes finding time to notice the very first crocus of the year. It's not a bad life if you're strong of heart.

To Contemplate

- What is the state of your creativity right now in relationship to the age(s) of your child(ren)? Are you expecting more of yourself than might be possible, given the ages and stages you're experiencing? Can you find a few things to enjoy about this current stage, while also looking ahead to new possibilities that await you?

Wise Words

"Because my teenage son spends the school year with his dad, I doubly enjoy the time I have with him. I don't have the luxury of experiencing my kid slamming through the door every afternoon asking what's for dinner, but in the summer when he's with me, I get to go into his room when he's sleeping and pull the covers over him. Believe me, I appreciate it!"
—Clarice Williams

"Life has shifted now that my own kids are so much older. I can truly enjoy the young children I teach. It makes me nostalgic, and fills that pocket for me. I get to deal with babies and two-year-olds—whom I adore. The whole world is magic when you're two!"
—Christy Cutler

"What I hear from my friends is that you don't realize that you're doing a better job than you think you're doing. And the creativity will come back to you when you have more time."
—Wendi Schneider

Part Two

The Path

Chapter Six

Self-Care and the Creative Woman

"One of the first and most invaluable possessions we lose when overstressed is time for creativity and leisure."

—Alice D. Domar, Ph.D.
Self-Nurture: Learning to Care for Yourself as Effectively as You Care for Everyone Else

O f the dozens of questions I asked the normally bright and articulate women in this book, one in particular seemed to cause temporary mumbling, rapid blinking, noticeable confusion and prolonged silence. The question was a simple one—*"What do you do to take care of yourself?"*—yet it brought out complicated feelings and responses each time I ventured to ask.

Maria Katzenbach looked me in the eye and said, **"The honest answer is that I'm real bad at that, and I'm trying to get better."** Dee Paddock stared at the ceiling and admitted, **"I don't do a very good job of that."** Christy Cutler studied her notes and stammered, **"Let's see, what did I put down here . . . ? Oh,** white space!" Gracie Carr shook her head and then blurted, "I'm not sure."

Now, with further probing, each woman offered wonderful examples of things she does to nurture her body, soul, and creative spirit. But the fact that it takes any probing at all exposes the guilt and reluctance women feel toward taking time for self-care. And it's not as if we don't all know how important self-care is in maintaining our health, our relationships, our emotional equilibrium, and our essential creative essence. Our doctors tell us this, as do our therapists, our partners, our friends, and even our mothers. We've all read the endless articles in magazines about the disastrous results of too much stress in our lives, and too little fun and leisure: cancer, heart disease, depression, divorce, loneliness, isolation, and anxiety, just to name a few.

We know we should certainly take as good care of ourselves as we do our children, our pets, our plants, our car, our home, and every single other person on the planet for whom we feel responsible. So why the hesitation in divulging our self-care secrets?

I think it's because women in general and mothers in particular believe that self-care means self-centeredness and self-indulgence (which are certainly frowned upon!), and that the most rewarding thing we can do is to spend every second of our lives in self-sacrificing service to others. Oh, the endless ways that the tiny word "self" can be plunked down in front of other words and become an instant messenger of doom.

In her book *The Sacrificial Mother*, Carin Rubenstein, Ph.D., gives example after painful example of mothers who don't believe they have a self worth caring for and spend their lives in servitude to their offspring and others. Though she uncovers legitimate historical, cultural and even biological imperatives for this kind of behavior, she drives home an important message about the effects of this pattern of sacrifice on the health of mothers *and* the well-being of their children:

> While it may come as a terrible shock to sacrificial mothers who are afraid of selfishness, women who can focus on themselves are much better off than those who can't. Selfish mothers are happier and healthier than sacrificial mothers. They even view themselves as more successful wives, mothers, and lovers. Women who are selfish get immediate benefits, such as being in good physical shape because they take time to exercise, or being well-informed because they take time to read newspapers or books, or being more relaxed because they find time to meditate or do yoga. But they also get permanent, lifelong blessings, because it's easier for them to live their lives as well.

To this, I would add one further distinction—that selfish women have more energy, fire and inspiration to throw into their creative work because they are rested and rejuvenated and take appropriate breaks from mothering and caretaking. To create at all, we must have a deeply vested interest in the workings of our one and only, absolutely unique *self*. To deny self is, ultimately, to deny creativity.

So, in the spirit of becoming happy and healthy selfish women, I'm thrilled to offer you The Big Purple Mommy ABC's of Self-Care, an encyclopedia of indulgent ideas compiled from the *repeated probing* (you can't imagine) of all the women you've met so far. Some of these ideas will undoubtedly be familiar to you, and may already be a part of your self-care ritual. Others may seem new and intriguing and perhaps worth a try. Whatever the case, the important thing is to choose one or two (or more!)

each day and practice self-care with the same dedication you practice caring for others.

The Self-Care Alphabet

A is for having the **attitude** that you have a self worth caring for. This is extremely important, for without this basic belief, no amount of superficial pampering can make a difference in your health and happiness.

B is for **baths**, a favorite among our interviewees. Many women sing the praises of a daily (or nightly) bath, especially with the added extras of candlelight, special soaps and oils, a glass of wine or cup of tea, and a half hour to soak and luxuriate. This is not, you understand, a family bath. No children allowed. Just you, your bubbles, and some well-deserved bliss. (If your children are small and have a hard time understanding this concept, have them read the picture book *Five Minutes Peace* by Jill Murphy.)

A close second to baths is the slightly fantastical notion of finding and keeping a regular and dependable Saturday night **babysitter** with all the qualities of Mary Poppins and an MA in early childhood education. Sorry to be the voice of reason here, but you have a better chance with the bath.

C means **coffee** to many women, and they don't mean microwaving yesterday's dregs for a desperate dose of caffeine. They mean taking a break and heading to their favorite neighborhood coffee bar for a double, non-fat, extra hot latte with a shot of vanilla, no foam (or whatever your signature drink may be). Part of the pleasure here, besides getting *exactly* what you want for just a moment, is getting out of your office or studio or living room and connecting with the adult human population.

The hubbub of voices, the gleaming pastry case, the swirl of activity—all of this can feel downright exciting after a morning work session or an afternoon with children.

D is for **dancing**, one of my personal favorites. You might be surprised how many women admit to turning up the music full throb and dancing around the house—with or without children. Dancing not only produces those magnificent endorphins we all need, but it also helps release tension and anger in our overtaxed bodies. Personally, I get a kick out of humiliating myself in front of my daughters by showing them my favorite nerdy disco steps, straight out of *Saturday Night Fever*.

You might try the kind of dancing Jahnna Beecham likes— the kind where she and her husband leave the kids with a sitter and take classes in ballroom and swing! She says it's one of the few things they do just for them, that doesn't involve children or careers.

Exercise made the top of our list as the most popular form of self-care. From blading to power lifting, from biking to hiking, we're out there moving our bodies. Not only are we trying to stay fit and healthy, we believe in the power of exercise to reduce stress and increase mental clarity. Many women report that creative ideas flow while they're exercising—shapes, colors, words, connections, concepts. If I'm feeling stuck in a particular project, exercise seems to nudge me toward a sense of creative freedom. Maybe it's as simple as more oxygen to the brain, maybe it's that weird gel in my running shoes. But it works!

Food. Now before you get worried and think that we're telling you to eat your way to happiness, or eat to mask unhappiness, just think about the self-care involved in preparing and eating good food. Nothing speaks to taking care of yourself like the essential act of making homemade soup, of cutting a slice of ripe tomato and eating it with a sprinkle of salt, or nibbling on a raisin scone during a mid-morning break. Or how about scouring the farmer's market or neighborhood health store for something fresh and delicious? And then there's the glory of reading those fat, glossy cookbooks you'll never buy in your favorite bookstore. We give you permission to browse through exotic ethnic markets, sample delicacies from the gourmet section of snooty department stores, and yes, occasionally indulge in that plate of to-die-for onion rings at the greasy diner on the corner.

And if you don't feel like cooking your own food, going out to dinner definitely counts as food-related self-care. Let someone else do the work—just feed your body and feed your soul.

Grooming is an ancient staple of self-care and includes a wide variety of rejuvenating treatments for our skin and hair. Our foremothers and foresisters crushed berries to tint their skin and used henna to add color and shine to their locks. On one end of the spectrum is Moira Keefe, who tells me that she tries to shave her legs "about every four weeks when the neighbors start to complain," and then there are women who save their pennies for regular manicures and facials. Whether you treat yourself at a spa or salon or do it yourself at home, enjoy a polish, peel, wax, weave, scrub, or scalp treatment today. It's not that creative mothers are overly vain; we just understand the benefits of not looking and feeling like neglected, bedraggled moms who don't deserve a little sparkle.

H brings us two fabulous ideas: **Hibernating** and **hiring a housecleaner.** The best break for many women is simply hunkering down at home for some "pulling in" time, away from the pressures and demands of the outside world. Hibernating may or may not include comfortable p.j.'s, unplugging the phone, a bowl of popcorn, a stack of unread magazines and the family dog at your feet.

Some women tell me they happily forgo all other indulgences

in order to be able to afford someone else to sweep up all that spilled popcorn and dog hair. A weekly or twice monthly house-cleaner is an absolute priority for some, and an ongoing fantasy for others. But everyone agrees—if you can afford it, hiring a housecleaner frees much more time for both creative work and family life.

Giving ourselves permission to enjoy small **indulgences** is a relatively inexpensive but wildly effective form of self-care. We feel taken care of when we let ourselves partake of some of life's little luxuries. The possibilities are endless, but our interviewees recommend fresh flowers, a nice bottle of champagne (for no particular reason), a new perfume, some gorgeous stationery and a sleek pen, travel books, the best chocolate you can find, a pair of funky earrings—you get the idea. Clarice Williams tells me that after weeks of rehearsing a play in another city, she and other cast members used their day off to travel to an outlying mall, just for the fun of buying new lipstick. Now, we all know that a new shade of lip color won't solve our problems, but it sure makes us lighten up for a little while.

Writing in a **journal** can be a soothing activity that helps us recognize the beauty of our unfolding lives. Many women spend time each day chronicling their dreams, ideas, plans, and deepest desires. Writing about the events of the past, along with day-to-day experiences and our hopes for the future, can be an invaluable tool for knowing ourselves and understanding our choices.

Our **kin** and extended family can help us feel connected to a larger community than that of our individual family unit. The web of our parents and cousins and aunts and uncles and in-laws and siblings, as well as those people we "choose" as family, can add value and meaning to our lives. It's not just the shared history and intimacy we like, it's the sense of being known and accepted. (And if your own web of relations is too tangled and sticky to offer you any nurturing or comfort, you might want to scan down to **T** for **therapy!**)

Ah, and now let's talk about **love** as a delicious discipline of self-care. And we're talking any and all forms of the above ("whatever floats your boat," as my daughter says). Whether you give it and get it from your partner, your children, your friends, your cat, or the entire global community, that lovin' feeling is one of the best available potions for burnout and stress. The more you give, the more you get, so don't save it all for Valentine's Day.

And the runner up to love for our creative women is **laughter.** They urge us to laugh at ourselves, laugh at the world, laugh with our children, or be a purist and laugh with the Marx Brothers, Lucille Ball, and the stand-up comedians at your local club. Go ahead—laugh at the stupid jokes your brother forwards to your e-mail, and the knock-knock joke your five-year-old tells you that contains more pieces of fruit than you can keep track of. It's good for you—it might help prevent disease—and it doesn't cost a dime.

Going to the **movies** was the big winner here, followed by **music, meditation,** and **massage.** Wendi Schneider says her favorite escape is to head off to a matinee—alone. She doesn't mind paying a sitter to watch her son, because the visual stimulation and diversion are worth the price. "It can be an expensive afternoon," she says, "but it reminds me of my New York days when I went to movies all the time!"

Listening to **music,** singing along to music, and playing an instrument are all activities that bring pleasure and relaxation. Aisha Zawadi tells me that when she can't paint, she puts on music "and sings for hours and hours." Jahnna leaves instruments around the house (including a harp) for everyone to enjoy.

Though she doesn't know how to play the harp, she says simply plucking the strings is greatly relaxing.

Meditation is a must for many creative women, especially at the very start of the day when they can grab a few quiet moments to themselves. It can clear the cobwebs from a sleepy brain and leave you feeling calm and centered. Personally, I'm indebted to my **massage** therapist, Mary, who works wonders on the knots that develop in my neck, shoulders, and back after hours spent in front of a computer. Twice a month I actually combine all of the **M's**—I listen to music and meditate while Mary performs her magic.

We all crave a **night out**—away from the house, the kids, our work, our responsibilities. Whether it's a carefully planned event or a totally spontaneous happening, a night out can feel like a mini-vacation. Christy Cutler says she's replenished by attending concerts and plays, and that the other artistic disciplines feed the creativity in her own dancing. When my children were very small, my husband and I would often plan to see a movie but end up missing it because it was somehow impossible to get out of the house once the sitter arrived. Sometimes, we actually ended up grocery shopping or doing mindless errands, which at the time seemed heavenly because at least we were together and out of the house. Lately, it seems we spend a great deal of time taking our hormonal daughters to school dances, after spending the day shopping for dresses and shoes and watching them fuss with their hair and makeup. This leaves me with serious longings for a night of dancing myself, complete with a new dress and shoes. Granted, middle-aged hormones are a different thing altogether, but I'm determined not to let the teenagers have all the fun!

There's no friend like an **old friend** to pick up our spirits and make us laugh. Nothing is quite as wonderful as a lunch or dinner with our best pal, complete with serious conversation and silly gossip. When you need someone to remind you that you're doing just fine and that your life looks pretty good, get together with a friend who can give you some perspective and encouragement. What would we do without them, those patient, enduring, fabulous people?

P.S. If you were looking for **orgasm**, by any chance, look under **S** for sex!

Hanging out with our **pets** can be a terrific source of self-care. Let's face it, they love us unconditionally, they don't find it necessary to share their every thought, and they're warm and furry. They're also very funny—watching my dog chase squirrels in her sleep is hugely amusing. We've all heard the news that just petting a dog or cat can lower our blood pressure and slow our breathing.

Q is for—you guessed it—absolute **quiet.** An absence of voices and noises is what many of us crave, and in fact, require in order to truly take care of ourselves. The cacophony of sounds that swirl around us throughout a typical day can cause an aural overload and leave us feeling tense and anxious. The pure joy of an hour of quiet time to regroup, rest, or simply putter around is an underrated gift.

And speaking of quiet time—the way many of us like to enjoy those stolen moments is with a good book. **Reading** ranks high as a coveted pleasure, and many of the women I interviewed belong to monthly book groups. These groups not only provide intellectual stimulation, but much needed social interaction, too. Dee Paddock says that she always makes time for reading because "it fills me up and gives me new stories."

Rituals give us a structure for self-care by allowing us to celebrate the beauty of ordinary life, as well as special occasions and holidays. The turn of the season, the cycle of the year, the beginning and end of each day can be acknowledged through individually designed rituals. Why not invent your own ritual to honor the small steps and giant leaps of your creative life?

S is by far the largest category of self-care—a virtual anthology that includes **sex, sleep, solitude,** and **spiritual life.** Note that these can be enjoyed one at a time, or in whatever order and combination you choose! Not everyone was willing to talk about the joy of sex, but Gracie Carr says that sex is definitely on her list because, "It validates my womanhood and makes me feel alive and creative."

Sleep hardly needs an endorsement, nor does **solitude.** Without these commodities we're apt to become cranky, rigid, depressed, and anxious. I notice that after a period of too little sleep, my most beloved family members are likely to become the victims of my slow but seething . . . shall we say *irritation*? A friend of mine tells me that when she's sleep-deprived, the voices of her children begin to sound like malnourished goats and she contemplates contracting an exotic but curable disease, just so she could lie in a small, clean bed and sleep for several weeks.

Spirituality soothes our soul, reminding us of the solace to be found in connecting with a larger creative force in the universe. Depending on our beliefs, spiritual practice helps us keep a balanced perspective in a chaotic world, and reminds us to indulge in daily gratitude. Prayer, chanting, meditation, visualization—all of these foster acceptance and tranquility—and ultimately, an enhanced sense of well-being.

Many creative women are drawn to the growth and discovery that comes from working with an attuned **therapist.** The therapeutic process has numerous rewards, including making peace with a difficult past, overcoming abuse and addiction, understanding a complex relationship, and recognizing our underlying motivations and patterns. And just the relief of having an hour a week with which to pour out the jumbled contents of our soul to an impartial person is a mighty fine thing, indeed. Forget ink blots and Freudian slips—think increased awareness and the potential for greater happiness.

Be an **underachiever**, just for one day. (This is especially helpful if you don't have a therapist or your therapist is out of town!) Set your sights low and be content to just get through the day. No beating yourself up for falling short of a goal, shouting at your kids, or letting a commitment slip. We're talking about just one day—not your whole life—so eat some high-fat, forbidden snacks, walk around with unwashed hair, forget to exercise, don't call your mother, watch a talk show, take a nap, let your children have frozen waffles for dinner, and vow to be perfect tomorrow. Just one Underachiever Day a quarter can change your life and remind you how it felt to be a college freshman.

Vacations take us away from the routine of our daily lives and shake things up a bit. New sights, sounds, smells and tastes stimulate our creativity and get us thinking in different ways. If you live near the ocean but never see the mountains, consider an alpine experience. Are you a city woman yearning for a rural respite? What would happen if you traded the forest for the plains, just for a week or so? So you can't afford Europe or Hawaii or the raft trip this year—what's happening within a hundred-mile radius of your home that might give you a memorable creative boost? Planning and enjoying vacations is an art form in itself, so it makes sense to keep practicing as often as you can.

Taking a **walk** is a simple but rewarding way to take care of ourselves. Almost every woman I talked to spoke of the importance of a daily walk—and not a calorie-burning, power-building kind of walk, either. Just a relaxing, meandering, take the dog or stroller along sort of walk, where we're free to notice the world around us, feel the sun on our face, and let our thoughts wander. I have a ritual walk that I take with my dog to a local park, and almost always by the time I'm halfway around the park I've uncovered a fresh idea or a possible solution to a nagging problem. Plus, my dog is sweetly grateful, which makes it all worth it.

X. Oh, forget it!

Many women practice **yoga,** which keeps their bodies stretched and limber and their minds refreshed. All that focused breathing and slow movement is a natural antidote to the frenzied pace of our days. If you can't get to a yoga studio, you can buy some wonderful video tapes for under ten dollars. My oldest daughter and I are hooked on a particular yoga tape led by an attractive, muscled man attired in a black bikini with a cool braid who demonstrates the Downward Dog on a pristine beach in Maui. We've been known to arise very early in the morning just to pop the tape in and hear him whisper, "Namaste," as the waves lap the white sands!

Z is for **zooming out,** widening the frame of our lens, and gaining perspective on our current circumstances. As my favorite bumper sticker so wisely proclaims, "Another Hundred Years, All New People." This gives me a strange solace, because it reminds me that whatever is causing me pain or concern will pass away, no matter how much I worry, fume or plot. Our children will grow through their difficult stages, we will move past the obstacles in our creative work, and everything in our lives will continue mutating, only to become brand-new again.

So, there you have it—at least thirty ideas for nurturing your self and your creativity. Hopefully, some of these are already a part of your self-care routine, and others will be added in the weeks and months to come. And don't forget that **believing you** have a self worth caring for is the most important ingredient of all.

To Contemplate

- How are you doing with self-care? Do you already partake in some of the suggested ABC's? Are there some you may be tempted to try in the near future? Did we leave out one of your personal favorites? Call one of your best friends and let her in on your secret.

Wise Words

This time, they've all been said!

Chapter Seven

Circle of Support

"Isolation is difficult for any human, whether
male or female, but for a woman it is what
psychologists call 'ego-dystonic,' or out of
tune with our accustomed way of being. For
that reason, it has the potential to be a
serious stress, despite the busyness of our
lives, we need to be mindful of the
continued need to support and be supported
by one another."

—Joan Borysenko, Ph.D.
A Woman's Book of Life

I n the previous chapter we looked at dozens of ways to take
good care of our physical, mental, emotional, and spiritual
health. And while we touched briefly on the importance of
friends and family to both our creative work and our mothering,
in this chapter we'll take a more detailed look at the individuals
and groups who form our very necessary circle of support. As
Dr. Borysekno points out, to be isolated from such support can
cause significant stress in our lives. And since we've already un-

covered the reality that both mothers and artists are naturally vulnerable to isolation—just because of the nature of the work—it's even more crucial for us to identify that strong, healthy community.

At first glance, it might seem a fairly easy task to identify the people who stand by us, are fond of us, and offer help and encouragement along our meandering paths. But because both motherhood and creative work are arenas within the human experience that seem to attract a great deal of competition, envy, and judgment, it's not always so simple and straightforward.

Consider the following scenarios:

Deena has been one of your best friends since the two of you met several years ago when your sons were in the same kindergarten class. Having children the same age gave you an instant bond. But now that the boys are older and in different classes, you don't feel quite as close. Besides, every time you mention your gallery show coming up in the spring, Deena looks slightly bored and turns the conversation in a different direction.

Freida thinks you're one of the most talented singers she's ever worked with, and you feel incredibly lucky to have landed her for a voice coach and teacher. While you love the way she pushes you to take your budding career more seriously, you're beginning to feel a bit pressured. She wants you to perform more, and keeps reminding you about out-of-town opportunities. You keep reminding HER that you have a six-month-old, and traveling isn't possible for you right now. She doesn't have children, and you get the strong impression she doesn't understand your feelings.

You hate to admit it, even to yourself, but your husband isn't all that supportive of your creative work. All you want to do when the kids are finally asleep is to have a couple of quiet hours in which to work on your novel. But he makes it clear that he wants you to stay in the living room and talk with him, watch television, and hang out. When you refuse, he acts hurt and sullen and you find yourself growing increasingly resentful.

We've all experienced situations similar to these, when it's not exactly clear if we're being supported or not. And because our double priority of creating and mothering causes us to feel varying amounts of guilt, we're often prone to blame ourselves for the lack of support in a given relationship. It's easier to tell ourselves that we're being picky and demanding too much from others than to see that maybe what we're getting back at times is negative and even hurtful. When the relationships are healthy and reciprocal, our friends, family, mentors and children can sustain us as mothers and creative women. Well-run groups and organizations can also provide invaluable support, networking opportunities, and education as we strive to grow as mothers and artists.

But because our time is overscheduled and our energy finite, we must carefully choose the composition of our support circle so that we're giving and getting a high percentage of love, understanding and encouragement. If there are relationships or groups in your life that continually drain and frustrate you, and put the damper on your creative fire, it may be time to reshuffle the Rolodex with a simple game of "Red Light, Green Light."

Red Light, Green Light

Remember playing this childhood game? The leader would call out a red, yellow, or green light with her back turned, only to quickly turn around and try to catch the players racing toward home and "speeding through a red." The thrill of trying to start and stop running on a dime while simultaneously gaining a winning distance was probably excellent training for our impending adulthood. It probably didn't help our driving skills, but I'll never forget the taste of victory when I successfully reached home base on a yellow before the caller could choke out the dreaded "red light" command.

Using those three familiar stoplight colors is a very simple but helpful way to evaluate relationships and groups. While not complex, it gives you an instant snapshot of where things are in terms of mutual support and respect. Here's how I utilize this basic tool:

Green Light: People and groups in this category are full of positive, affirming energy. They give you the green light to be who you are, become what you dream, and you do the same for them. There are few limiting rules and confusing roles to understand. Green light friends love the creative work you do *and* support you as a mother—sometimes they even remind you to watch the speed limit!

Yellow Light: Your gut and heart feel a sense of caution around these people or groups. The flashing yellow makes you careful about what you say and how much you reveal of your true spirit. Always aware that the light could change to red at any moment, you feel somewhat tense and uneasy. You're unclear about how you're perceived as a mother and creative woman. Yellow light folks are more likely to be acquaintances, neighbors and business associates than true friends.

Red Light: Stop. Put on the brakes. Proceed no farther. Red light people and groups make it clear that your progress should be halted. There is little flexibility, trust, or humor here. You have the sense of strong judgment being leveled at you as a mother and creative woman. The punishment for inching forward in your life can be harsh. Red light people come disguised as friends, lovers, teachers, even family members, which makes it all even trickier.

Of course, not every person or situation can be easily fitted into these broad categories, and we all recognize that dozens of subtle shades exist on the spectrum between green, yellow, and red. Circumstance, history, objectives and needs give a specific and often changing hue to all of our relationships. But for a quick assessment, "Red Light, Green Light" is a good place to start (and works well when talking to our children about their feelings for their friends).

Intimate Partners

For some of us, our significant other is the most intimate and important person in our circle of support. Because these men and women are our partners in daily life, and in parenting our children, they often play a huge role in helping us realize our creative dreams. A number of the women I interviewed named their partner as the person they most depend on for love and support.

Jahnna Beecham says, "My husband, Malcolm, is the rock in our group. In our world, he's the one who packs the lunches and makes sure the kids get off to school on time."

Christy Cutler reports, "Bill has supported my dance career all along. Whenever I start thinking it's not much, he'll say, 'You run a business! You do this and that! You're an entrepreneur!' We all need to hear these things over and over again."

Lady McCrady sings the praises of her husband, Martin. "He's practical when I'm not, and vice versa. Luckily, he loves food (and cooking and shopping). If not for this, my children and I would not be so comfortable, so healthy, so self-assured and vital. He's charming and funny and surprising—and he also does the laundry."

These are clearly green light partners, who help facilitate big dreams while also sharing in the small but necessary chores of raising children and living in a home. Not surprisingly, the women with these kinds of partners are likely to hear a drowning chorus of, *"You're so lucky! How did you get so lucky?"* when they describe their relationships.

But believe me, luck seems to have little to do with it. Creative women know in their bones that their ability to thrive depends on recognizing the nurturing characteristics in a potential partner. These women will tell you that they made very conscious choices about partnership and marriage based on their beloved's willingness to be directly involved in homemaking, child rearing, and the support of mutual dreams and goals. Creative women need to be as creative in building and sustaining strong, equitable relationships as they are in their individual work.

Meet Michele

Michele Bograd is a family therapist, writer, teacher, and facilitator who lives in the Boston area. Her partner, Tom, is also a therapist who works as an elementary school counselor, and together, they are raising a school-aged son and daughter.

Though Michele is accomplished and noted in her field, has published a number of articles and papers, and edited several books, she takes pains to play down her creativity. She muses about whether this stems from the intellectual work of women being marginalized, or because the play of rich ideas comes so easily to her that she dismisses its worth. She does concede, though, that, "Other people see me as being very intellectually creative."

In our interview, Michele spoke candidly about the importance of choosing the right partner in achieving the life you dream.

> I have a partner who is extremely supportive. We can work out what I need as far as my creative work, and sometimes it requires a lot of negotiation. I can sometimes feel guilty or conflicted about the time I need away from the family, so then it's really important to have a partner who helps you get done what you need to get done without resenting you for it. Primarily, if you're partnered, you need someone who supports your work and will be a willing co-parent. I find I can't work when the kids are around—they won't let me work. Having an active partner frees me up to do my work, and frees me of my guilt.
>
> Because I'm a feminist, I have certain beliefs about how to mother, what I want my marriage to look like, and what I need from my marriage to allow me to develop intellectually and creatively.

I asked my husband if he could articulate why it's important for men to actively support their partners' creative dreams. His answer was so inspiring that I decided to include him as the one and only male voice in this book. Here's Larry, spokesman for

Men Who Support Creative Women—an organization that desperately needs to become a real entity:

> The support, or lack thereof, speaks to the heart of equality in a relationship. If I failed to support my partner, I'd be failing my own deep sense of fairness. Men get a surplus of support from their partners and the culture, while women traditionally get relegated to First Lady status. Well, it doesn't take a genius to understand what happens to a marriage if one person is thwarted or frustrated in her dreams. If a man's ego is so fragile and petty that it necessitates keeping "the little woman in her place"—well, then that man's a perpetual adolescent—he's not a grownup.

I promise I didn't put words in Larry's mouth. In my second marriage I had the wisdom and intuition (no, it's *not* just luck) to choose a smart and evolved man with whom to share my life.

Mothers without Partners

Not everyone has, or chooses to have an intimate partner with whom to raise her children. The family configurations that evolve beyond the traditional model are numerous and varied, colorful and intriguing. For instance, Maria Katzenbach is raising her son in tandem with her former husband in an arrangement that ultimately gives her a better structure for her creative work. But she had to be creative in identifying what she needed and asking her former husband to help.

During an intense time in Maria's life when she was trying to finish a novel that was deeply meaningful to her, she realized that her best time for thinking and writing was in the quiet, near dream state of early morning. But as all mothers know, children have vastly different A.M. rhythms, and clamor for breakfast, companionship, conversation and attention almost from the moment they awaken. At the same time that Maria began to realize her need for morning solitude, she saw that her son wanted more time with his father. She decided to take a risk and see if their established calendar could be reshuffled to everyone's benefit.

> Eventually, I arranged it with my former husband so that I could get mornings free—but I had to ask for it. It's important to say that I had to assert that need. Now, I have complete time, three or four days a week. It's working for us, and there's this weird part of me that knows that because I'm divorced and share custody of my child, and because of an unconventional arrangement, I'm able to do sustained creative work. Partnered women don't always get that.

While Maria isn't advocating divorce as a pathway to creativity, she's quick to point out that being a single mother doesn't have to mean the death or postponement of creative dreams. It doesn't have to mean an absence of support for the adults and children involved. Maria took a situation that looks, at first glance, to be difficult and constraining and turned it into a mutually positive experience.

> It worked because our needs dovetailed. They were absolutely in sync, because my son needed to be with his dad more and I needed some freedom in the mornings. Courage came from telling myself that it is part of a parent's responsibility to show our children what realizing a dream and fulfilling a destiny really takes. If I did not ask for what I

needed, my son, who is highly creative, would be at risk for not asking when his own time comes.

Maria says that her current support circle consists mainly of her friends and family, especially her parents. "My mom and dad have given me more support than anyone else," she says. Both Aisha and Clarice, who are also single mothers, agree that in the absence of a primary partner, close friends and family become especially important.

Family Support

Our web of family and extended family can be a rich source of support. Depending on proximity and circumstance they can offer companionship, advice, financial help, and a long list of practical aid, such as babysitting and chauffeuring our children, and helping prepare for holidays and celebrations. Best of all, our family can provide comfort and emotional connection in our vast, global community.

This, I fully realize, is a best-case scenario or even a Hollywood fantasy for some. Many women confess that they're more likely to get the love and support they need from friends, neighbors, and complete strangers than they are from their family of origin. If this is the case for you, skip right ahead to the other areas of support and don't look back. And if this is a place of raw and ongoing hurt for you, it's probably not a bad idea to seek the help of a great therapist. You may discover new information about the origins of your creativity as you wrestle with the past. A dear friend of mine who is separated geographically and emotionally from her family is just now realizing that she was always meant to be a teacher, rather than the nurse her father pressed her to become.

If you *do* have loving family around who adore your children and think you're creatively gifted, rejoice in your abundance and continue to find ways to keep them in your story. My mother and sister occupy irreplaceable positions in my circle of support, as do my mother-in-law and sisters-in-law. Without them, my life and my children's lives would be less bright. This isn't to say, of course, that we don't struggle to stay close, sometimes disagree, and even, at times, cross boundaries and step foot where we ought not go. I've perpetrated and endured slammed doors, months of bitter silence, ugly grudges, and once, an ongoing argument about the dangers of freezing most dairy products. But I know that a helping hand or patient ear is only a phone call away, and for that I count my lucky stars.

Friends

For most women, our friends make up the biggest portion of our support circle, surrounding us with the kind of nurturing that only comes from true familiars. Some women sustain friendships with childhood friends, relying on phone calls, e-mail, and letters to keep in touch across states and continents. Others feel most connected to friends made in adulthood, and most of us can identify a series of transitional friendships that are part of a specific job or creative project, or emerge during a specific stage in our life.

Especially as women raising children and working in creative fields, transitional friendships may be the rule rather than the exception. For example, we may be drawn to certain women we meet through our child's preschool, but lose contact when the children scatter to different kindergarten programs. We may form an instant and intense bond with someone we meet in our ten-week printmaking class, only to discover later that the friendship never cements outside of class.

I used to feel confused and somewhat guilty over these serial friendships, wondering if I lacked the gene for sustained relationships. But the more women I talk to about this, the more I've been able to relax. It seems that most women experience this same dance of attachment and detachment over and over again as their children grow and their creativity unfolds in new ways. Being mothers today is a little bit like being in the military—our children change schools, teams, and Girl Scout groups with the same frequency that we move to different neighborhoods, jobs, and churches. We're all in constant motion, moving along pathways that bring us in contact with hundreds of other adults and children who are moving along their own busy paths. Mostly we wave, smile, and occasionally share a cup of coffee or the intriguing thread of a conversation before we're on our way again.

It gives me more than a twinge of sadness to realize how temporal our membership in communities can be. But the good news is that *every once in a while*, a true friendship sparks and ignites between two people at one of these crowded intersections—one that beats the odds and outlasts all future wandering.

When you're lucky enough to have that happen in your life, hold on tightly to your friend and rejoice. The powers working in the universe have given you a green light for joy.

Other Mothers

I can't leave the subject of female friendship without hesitating for a moment and bringing up the elephant in the room that none of us like to acknowledge—our complicated relationships with other mothers. When I was young and hadn't yet touched the fire, I think I assumed that all women, and especially women raising children, shared a common and sacred bond. I believed, innocently, that we were members of a tribe, a respected club that required that we treat each other with tenderness and respect.

I've learned through hard experience that the mere shared characteristic of being mothers has little to do with tenderness and respect. It can, and certainly *should*, foster our best mutual qualities, but this is often not the case. In the past few years, I've experienced the painful death of a longtime friendship because of petty maternal gossip that ultimately resulted in my inability to trust a once important friend. And while I've been the target of such unpleasantness, I also know that I've participated in my share of unfair and debasing discussions about other mothers, their children, and their choices. As I've grown older and more confident as a woman and mother, I'm less likely to be drawn into damaging "mom talk" with other women. But if we're honest, most of us will admit that the temptation always exists.

Dee Paddock believes that power and competition often undermine our ability to support one another, and that the seemingly endless rift between traditional (meaning "stay-at-home") and non-traditional mothers (working outside) is more often than not at the heart of the problem:

> Some of this comes from my own issues, but I've never believed that other mothers will support me. Mothers can be viciously competitive. For many women who are traditional mothers, so much rides on how they are viewed in that one role. They need to show the world their superior children. I think that women are socialized to believe that motherhood is the appropriate realm for us to be competing in. Success is measured by what kind of child we produce.

It's also about power. Women who don't believe they have a lot of personal power want to get it by being the Best Mom on the Block. And then there's the element of fear. If I tell you that my daughter is having difficulty making friends, you might judge me for not teaching her some necessary social skill and let me know that I somehow didn't work hard enough to help her make friends.

Michele Bograd, who says that she's still "shocked by the vehemence on both sides of the working mom stay-at-home mom debate," says that she's almost reluctant to talk about relationships between mothers for fear of setting up even more division among the camps. But she, too, feels the loss of a community of supportive mothers.

I had this mythic sense that there was a community of mothers that I should be a part of. It's a "should" left over from the 1950's—I "should" be active in my community, the kids' school, and do "mom speak." But I find "mother talk" either unengaging to me personally, or I feel horrible that I'm not good at it. There's something out there for other mothers that I'm not able to do.

Entire books have already been written about the "mommy wars," and I feel inadequate in bringing much freshness to the tired debate. But I should add that a good friend recently pointed out that competition and power games aren't solely the domain of the opposing factions of working and stay-home moms. Lola, who formerly ran a busy non-profit arts agency, and has been home for a number of years raising her two daughters, informs me that the same withholding of support happens within groups of at-home mothers, as they vie for perceived superiority.

We're all so hungry for validation about our choices, and for how we're raising our children and living our lives. And because we're afraid of the reaction we might get if we disclose honest feelings about our lives, we just don't risk it. It's easier to distance yourself from others than to reach out. It's about sizing yourself up against others—a kind of placement method within the group. And there is power in withholding validation and therefore seeming superior.

And if all of this leaves you feeling overwhelmingly depressed at the state of mother-to-mother bonding, keep in mind that many women have completely opposite and very positive experiences creating trusting, non-judgmental bonds with fellow mothers.

Moira Keefe, whom I think of as a bridge builder, has a true gift for bringing mothers together and helping us celebrate our commonality rather than our differences. The first time I ever met her was when she invited me (in person, at my front door!) to a neighborhood gathering of mothers. She's famous all over the country for a unique event she's dubbed Moms and Margaritas.

The simplicity of the idea is what gives it its absolute brilliance—Moira makes up several huge thermoses of margaritas, opens her house and backyard, and invites everyone to bring snacks and kids and come hang out on a Friday afternoon.

Maybe it's the tequila; maybe it's the Mardi Gras-like atmosphere created by the large crowd and the non-stop laughter. But without fail, after a half-hour at one of her parties, the divisions between mothers seem to drop away like the crumbs of taco chips spilled on the kitchen floor. We become, at least momentarily, a big, happy family of faintly tired women just trying to get through our days and keep our children safe and healthy. We laugh at ourselves and each other, and amazingly intimate stories begin to pour forth from previously recalcitrant mothers.

I think Moira should be given the equivalent of a Mother Theresa award for the work she does to create common ground. And I think that if each of us followed suit and threw a similar party on a regular basis, we could probably change the face of mother-to-mother relationships. Perhaps we could all leave our baggage at the door and give each other the support we need and deserve. (And tequila makers everywhere would unite to make Moira the international spokesperson for fermented cactus libations and we'd all live happily ever after!)

Friends from the Creative Realm

Friends who share our passion for creative work are essential members of our support circles. This doesn't mean that if we paint we should only hang out with other painters, or that if we dance we should seek support only in the world of dance. But knowing other women and men (ah, a break from the intensity of female friendship!) who function in the creative realm gives us a community of like-minded people who understand our dreams and challenges firsthand.

I'm not suggesting that your dear friend the tax law attorney can't be sympathetic to your struggle with the ending of a song you're composing, or that your sister the computer genius won't be able to understand that you can't find a character for the woman you're playing on stage. It's just that it's sometimes so nice to sit down with a fellow creator and exchange stories of our process in a shared language that requires no translation. And often, these friendships are quite separate from our maternal life, and therefore bring out completely different sides of our selves.

A warning: friendships in the creative realm can produce just as much competition and envy as mother-to-mother relationships. Trust your gut if you feel a yellow or red light shining on the interaction. If you can openly celebrate your successes (not just your losses) and be met with true support from a creative friend, it can be one of the most validating experiences of all.

If you don't currently have friends from the creative realm, a good place to begin looking is through the wide variety of groups and organizations that exist solely to support artists and creators.

Group Life

I used to proudly proclaim that I just wasn't "a group person" and that I didn't particularly like societies, leagues, and clubs of any sort. I was never a Girl Scout or sorority sister, and I never owned any badges or pins that spoke of membership. I certainly never whispered a secret password or learned a sacred handshake. I liked my pattern of isolated work followed by casual socialization.

But then I turned forty and the isolation started to get to me. And casual socializing usually meant that I called someone, made the plans, bought the tickets or cooked the dinner. I floundered for a time until a friend suggested I join a group. The "G" word—I couldn't believe it. I turned this over and over in my mind and then made a decision. Within six months I would join two groups—one that already existed officially, and one that I would help create on my own. I figured that way I'd have both the control and the absolution of control that I truly crave.

I looked around at the writing groups already established in my city and settled on a large author's league organization that offered monthly events and speakers. Though I haven't attended more than a handful lately, I enjoy the camaraderie and networking when I go. Entering a roomful of working writers is like a kind of homecoming, and we're not even required to spit on the floor and turn around three times to the left under a full moon.

The second group I now belong to is a casual group of loosely connected women who meet once a month for dinner, lots of wine, and conversation. Some of us would never cross paths otherwise, and most of us are involved in some type of creative work. We're not a reading group, though we recently felt compelled to read and discuss a long book about Eleanor Roosevelt that we ended up loving. Sometimes we talk about politics, other books we're reading, and yes—our children. Again, I take great delight in these gatherings, and so far we haven't even discussed the possibility of wearing matching vests and earning badges.

Being in groups at this point in my life is teaching me to be open, to reach out in new ways, and not to fear that my tiny self can be swallowed whole in the presence of a group identity. If you're a confirmed non-groupie but longing for some fresh, creative friends to add to your circle, I recommend testing the waters of official and not-so-official organizations. You may surprise yourself.

Teachers and Mentors

This is a bit of a gray area, because teachers and mentors are often also our friends, family members, partners, fellow creators, and even our children. We may not even recognize who our mentors are until years and decades have passed. Let's face it—

we don't live in the kind of world where we have a weekly appointment with our mentor to discuss our creative hopes and dreams, fears, and nightmares. We don't usually have the luxury of apprenticing with an established creator who takes on the task of teaching us and guiding our careers. We don't often have a Merlin figure who shows us how to do magic and become a king.

But we do have those marvelous mere mortals who take time to show us, explain to us, suggest to us, and push us on our way like leaves in the wind. If you take a few minutes, you can probably list several people who function as your teachers right now. It might be your grandmother, your next-door neighbor, your college roommate, the woman who sells you your drawing paper at the art store. It might be the editor who opens a door for you, or the owner of the comedy club who patiently listens to your new routine and makes a brilliant suggestion. It might be the experienced mom down the street who shows you patience, or the aide in your son's classroom who can explain to you how your child learns numbers.

Whoever makes it on your list deserves much gratitude, and maybe even a bouquet of flowers from your garden. We aren't where we are because we did it all on our own, but because teachers came to us (in different forms) when we most needed them. And I'm learning along the way that the biggest debt of gratitude we can repay is by looking behind us and mentoring the quiet one standing there with wide, expectant eyes.

Our Children's Care Givers

The people who help us care for our children are a supremely important part of our support circle. Not only do they nurture and love our children while we're away or working, but they give us freedom to pursue our creative work.

As I write, our beloved, former babysitter is visiting for the weekend. She came into our lives when she was nineteen and my children were six, two, and two days old. She worked for us part-time for five years while she went to college, giving me mornings or afternoons to write. As the years went by, our relationship evolved to the point that Dana became an adored fixture in all of our lives—even when she no longer worked for us and went on to pursue her dream of becoming a nurse. With her youthful energy and zest for life, she helped me raise my daughters while I sometimes helped raise her. Though she is now grown up and married and living far away, she is an ongoing presence in our family, and an integral part of each of my daughters' life story.

Right now, Dana's in the backyard taking pictures of her older and taller former charges (she's a talented photographer) while they hold pieces of fruit on their heads. My oldest daughter sports a pineapple, while Natalie wears a crown of bananas. They are shrieking with an old and familiar kind of laughter, while I sit here marveling at the good fortune that brought her to us.

If you have a Dana, create a permanent space for her in the emotional life of your family. If you're searching for one, conjure every ounce of basic instinct you possess to recognize her among the crowd. Be prepared to deal with your own demons of control and occasional jealousy as she finds a way into your children's hearts. Understand that the complex web of relationships that can form from the simple act of hiring a caretaker will require respect and care and commitment with a capital C.

Most of all, know that the rewards of sharing the nurturing of your children with someone else can be abundant and ongoing.

Our Children

Last but not least in our circle of support are our very own children. It seems that no one loves us more, believes in us more, and supports our dreams with more innocent fervor than they do. My daughters have sat on the sofa and patted my back while I cried over an editor's rejection letter. They create heart-stopping screen savers on my computer that read: "*I Love You Mommy—Write Your Book!*" They brag about me to their friends and run to get a copy of one of my books the instant a guest walks through our door.

As they get older, my daughters read pieces of stories as I write them and offer surprisingly astute critiques. They help me think of character names, encourage me when I'm feeling blocked and stupid, and toast my progress. They are even savvy enough with computers to look up facts for me on Web sites. Though I don't have much excitement to offer them on "Take Your Daughter to Work Day"—(they'd rather go with an architect or pediatrician) they let me know that they're proud of how I spend my days.

I think that the more we let our children into the world of our creative work, the more opportunity they have to see the ups and downs of trying to stay true to a sometimes difficult path. The more we allow them to understand about our creative passion, the more room we give them to understand their own.

Giving Support

Because we've focused on looking at the configuration of our personal circle of support, I want to end by looking at how we *give* support to others. Take a moment and think about those people who count *you* among their supporters and teachers. Do you have creative friends to whom you offer encouragement as they pursue their work? Are there mothers in your circle who look to you for validation and comfort? Family members who depend on you for a sense of connection and history? Do you mentor a young student or cheerlead as your child takes tentative steps into the creative world?

Undoubtedly you sit strongly in dozens of circles, some of which overlap with your own circle and some of which stand far apart. Whatever the constellation, take care to notice the balance of giving and getting and aim for a flow of support that feels healthy and real—our mothering and creativity depend on it.

To Contemplate

• Who are the people (and groups) who make up your own circle of support? Write down names, if you like. Are there any obvious gaps? Are these "green light" people who support you as a mother or in your creative work? Who counts *you* among her circle of support? Are you giving "green light" validation and encouragement to these people?

Wise Words

"My children keep me from thinking I'm average!"
—Lady McCrady

"My support system contains a lot of people who don't have children, who are in non-traditionally shaped relationships—gay couples, a woman in her 50's who's never been permanently partnered. Be-

ing with them is one of the few places where I can
be both a mother and a professional. They under-
stand my struggle in both domains."
—Michele Bograd

"My friends support me as a creative person—
almost to the point of pressure, in a sense. If I
were to suddenly set my life up conventionally, I
think they would come to me and say, 'Are you all
right?' "
—Maria Katzenbach

Chapter Eight

The Time Thing

"To live is so startling it leaves little time for anything else."

—Emily Dickinson

Each time I interviewed a woman for this book, I asked the following question: *What three things do you most need in order to do your creative work?*

You probably won't be surprised to learn that "time" was at the top of everybody's list, placing first above such other commodities as quiet, solitude, energy, money, courage, babysitters, and coffee!

Having more time certainly tops my own list—in fact, to tell you the brutal truth, I don't actually have time to write this chapter. This is what my day is looking like:

It's 8:15 A.M. and my daughters have just left for school. In an hour I'm due at the doctor's office for my annual Pap smear, and before I go I need to finish the bean soup I started early this morning for tonight's dinner (in an attempt to save time, of course). At some point I have to shop for my father's late birthday present, go to the bank, get my hair cut, walk the dog, make a fund-raising poster for the 5th grade trip, clean off my desk, return about ten phone calls, pick up a book at the library, figure out why my car smells like a full Dumpster on a hot day, sign my oldest daughter up for driving school, and have a small, but complete mental breakdown. Oh, and did I mention I have a book chapter to write?

Just in case you were hoping that I have any answers about the time thing, I just want to tell you truthfully, right up front, that I don't. I'm probably better equipped to offer advice on how to torment squirrels so that they don't eat your tulip bulbs and birdseed, or how to squirt canned whipped cream into exactly even blobs on cups of hot chocolate so as to avoid a sibling war.

I struggle every day of my life with managing time, especially in the years since becoming a mother. While I have many insights to share from my interviews with other women, it seems "the time thing" is such a sprawling, all-encompassing topic that it probably should be a graduate-level degree program at institutions of higher learning. Indeed, the last time I checked the shelves at my local bookstore there were nearly fifty books devoted specifically to the subject.

And yet, as my interviews reinforced, the notion of time is such a strangely unique and personal thing that very few universal ideas apply. *Making time, using time, creating more time, finding the time, time passing by*—all of these mean different things to different people. And the way mothers *mark* time is vastly different from how children *feel* time and how creative women *experience* time. Personally, I always find myself using the more aggressive verbs when I talk about time. Instead of *making time*, I usually prefer descriptions like *capturing, wrestling, lassoing, stealing, grabbing, and outmaneuvering*. Which probably tells you something profound about my very relationship to the concept. I haven't *made friends with time*, or *tamed* it, or *caressed* it with loving hands.

Self-Care and Support Come before Time

One of the initial impetuses for this book actually arose out of a workshop I helped facilitate called, "Making Time For Creativity." A roomful of terrific women who were raising children and trying to do their creative work asked the panel (in about a dozen different ways) how it was possible in one crowded lifetime to make room for everything we want to do. Mostly we tossed out the tired and lame old answers about priorities and boundaries and learning to say no.

But in the year since that workshop, as I talked to more and more women and this book unfolded, I've slowly come to realize an important point—that to understand how we prioritize our time we first need to understand the concepts of self-care and circles of support. Because without the inner acknowledgment that we have selves worth caring for, and that we need and deserve the support of others, no advanced degree in time management can help us accomplish our creative work.

Making time can only happen when we know in our souls that our creative work is worth making time for. Making time can only happen when we're finally willing to ask others for help and support. Hopefully, since we explored both of these critical issues in the previous two chapters, we have a bit more of a context for plunging ahead and looking straight into the eyes of the time thing.

But when you feel yourself sliding into a time-induced depression, where it feels next to impossible to capture minutes or hours for your creative work, before you do anything else, take a breath and remember to ask yourself these two invaluable questions: **Do I believe, right this moment, that my creative work is a necessary expression of my soul that brings essential happiness to my life? Do I believe that I deserve the support of others in order to do my creative work?**

If the answer to either question is a resounding "no," remind yourself that you have issues to confront that are far more weighty than an absence of time.

Time Bites

Listen to what our interviewees have to say about time. No doubt you'll feel a sharp pang of recognition as you read their words.

"The major challenge is trying to find protected time. When I go into our upstairs office to work, the kids won't leave me alone, and in fact, I can't leave them alone. My ears are pricked up for them."
—Michele Bograd

"It's not just finding the time to do the work, but the time to be inspired and feel that creative urge again."
—Wendi Schneider

"Before motherhood, I had the time to work in a more consistent way. Sometimes I'd work eight

hours a day on a piece and it was an everyday ef-
fort. Now I work when I can, which is harder, be-
cause once I leave a piece, the energy and passion
isn't as strong when I get back to it. It's hard to re-
attach, especially if it's been a long period of time
in between."
—Aisha Zawadi

"Basically, before we had kids, our life was about
writing under a deadline. After kids, we had to begin
scheduling a 'real life,' which is better. We put our
writing into eight- to ten-hour days instead of
twenty."
—Jahnna Beecham

"I'm sort of a magnet when the kids are home. If I
sit down alone, they find me. I'm not good at say-
ing, 'I'm not available right now.'"
—Dee Paddock

"Time. Time. It's about deciding who is going to get
attention. I have every intention of going home every-
afternoon, playing piano, and writing down some
ideas. But those moments never happen. It's sud-
denly 10:00 P.M. and my day's over."
—Gracie Carr

Each of these brief musings describes a piece of the whole time pie for mothers who create. They speak to the wide array of challenges, including interruptions, transition time, getting sidetracked, organization, daydreaming time, managing domestic systems, procrastination, and time for the business details of creative work.

Before we look at each of these challenges in more detail, it might be helpful to first describe mother time, child time, and creative time.

Mother Time

As mothers, we tend to view time in a fairly traditional, straightforward way. Days are divided into predictable blocks that carry specific mother-related responsibilities. These can include preparing meals, helping children get ready for their day, driving to school and activities, homework, baths, bedtime, etc. They can also include the more engaging tasks of talking, snuggling, helping, listening, guiding, teaching, and protecting. In mother time, the days of the week follow a prescribed pattern, as do the months and even years. Though the pattern can be wonderfully interrupted by weekends, holidays, and summer, it mostly repeats itself like the brilliant but precise blocks of a quilt. Sometimes the minutes of mother time crawl by noticeably slower than "real" time, and sometimes they fly so fast you lose your breath.

Mother time is linear. It's black and white. It usually contains lists and agendas, which we adhere to for the well being of our children and for our own sanity. Following mother time can be exhausting, pressured, and downright boring—especially with multiple children. Mother time is a demanding master who must be served.

Child Time

Ah, child time . . . a way of marking time that is absolutely free of watches, alarms, calendars and "to do" lists. Child time is a great expanse of open sky, a bottomless pocket filled with all the best treats. The younger the child, the less dependent she is on our culture's linear model of time—we've all seen a three-year-old take seventeen glorious minutes to walk to the corner, stopping at whim to examine the rain gutter, half of a worm, and a flattened pine cone. And during that same seventeen minutes, we deluded adults will have adjusted our watch, made a mental note to have our tires rotated, picked up stray pieces of trash, planned the menu for the next three weeks of dinner, and tried to solve the mysteries of the universe, all the while urging our child to "hurry up."

Child time isn't clogged by competing agendas or future considerations. It exists purely in the miraculous "now." Even older children, like my nine-year-old Willa, don't have a firm grasp on the adult concept of time. When I wake her in the morning, she always asks me, sleepily, "Is this Tuesday or Wednesday? Do I have dance today?" I can't remember a time when I awoke not knowing exactly what day it was and what I had to accomplish.

Child time speeds by for our children when they're having a good time—a three-hour playdate seems like five minutes. And when they're counting the days until a birthday or holiday or summer vacation, time becomes the evil king blocking the treasure. Child time is a soaring kite, dipping unpredictably, slowing, zooming up again.

But mostly, as I'm sure you know, child time is the polar opposite of mother time—and that's where the daily struggle lies. We are continually trying to function in what amounts to a completely different realm from our children, urging them to join us in mother time while they are unable to leave the kingdom of child time.

Creative Time

And then there's creative time, which must answer to mother time and bears the best aspects of child time, but is its own entity altogether.

Creative time is almost a misnomer, because when we enter its gates, time ceases to exist. We look up several hours later, stunned to realize how fully engrossed we were and how linear time managed to loosen its hold on us. Creative time is almost like a drug. It pulls us in slowly, sometimes reluctantly, and then moment by moment we go deeper and deeper until we're feeling the full, euphoric effects. We forget to look at the clock, we no longer listen to distracting voices in our head, we aren't aware of the outside world, but only the hypnotic, hyper-attuned feeling of being connected to our creative soul.

When we are lucky enough to feel the "flow" of creative time, we can make remarkable things happen in our work. But it's not easy to access creative time when we're functioning on mother time. And our children, who are living in child time, don't understand that their natural inclinations to interrupt and reconnect destroy the delicate state of creative time.

Yet, I am aware that contained in all of this obvious disparity is perhaps the true time state of mothers who create. Within the spinning circles of mother time, child time, and creative time, we discover a fourth circle in the overlap—and out of default and need and invention, that fourth circle becomes our permeable home.

A Word about Transitions

In moving among the worlds of mother time, child time, and creative time, the transitions are bound to be bumpy. It's wise to expect this, and prepare for it as much as possible. If you've been doing creative work while your children are napping or in school, and you need to move into mother time—take a breath. Give yourself a moment to adjust to the next stage of your day. Do whatever you need to end one time experience—blow out the candle, stretch, put away supplies, make a few last notes, have a cup of tea—and enter the next.

If you're moving from mother time into creative time, try changing your clothes (you're going to work), putting on some music, eating a snack for energy—whatever you can do to access that other part of yourself.

And know that as you transition, so will your children. They may not like the way you seem changed or stirred up when you return to them. My children always look at me suspiciously when I stagger down my office stairs to the family room. They seem to be wondering where I've been, sensing that though I've been a few yards away, I've traveled far. Patience helps with transitions. So do hugs and cookies.

But know that it's a *good* thing for your children to see rapture on your face, and frustration, and confusion and glimpses of your creative self.

In an essay by Anne Tyler called "Still Just Writing," the author beautifully describes the process of transitioning:

> After the children started school, I put up the partitions in my mind. I would rush around in the morning braiding their hair, packing their lunches; then the second they were

gone I would grow quiet and climb the stairs to my study. Sometimes a child would come home early and I would feel a little tug between the parts of me; I'd be absent-minded and short-tempered. Then gradually I learned to make the transition more easily. It feels like a sort of string that I tell myself to loosen. When the children come home, I drop the string and close the study door and that's the end of it.

A Word about Interruptions

Fact: If you have children and you do your creative work somewhere inside your home, *you will be interrupted*. **Myth:** If you ask kindly enough and often enough, your children will respect your desires and leave you alone when it's your turn to work.

Okay, now that we've stated the obvious, how do we work around it? Here's where I feel like a passive panelist all over again, but there are only a few suggestions of any real value to offer. For instance, you can get up early, like Jahnna:

When things get overwhelming, if I can get up early and get two hours in before everyone else wakes up, I can really enter the day feeling I'm getting work done.

Or you can stay up late like Moira:

Sometimes I work late at night when everyone's asleep. I have a really big cup of coffee, work until 2:00, then get up at 6:00, and then take a nap in the afternoon before they all come home.

And if the thought of losing even a minute more of your already sketchy sleep is impossible to entertain, you can get a workspace outside of your home, padlock your current space and hire a great sitter, or you can learn to tolerate interruptions.

While I realize that none of these suggestions are wonderful (especially learning to live with constant interruption), I would be lying if I told you there are dozens of other creative solutions that you just haven't thought of. Interruptions are one of the most challenging aspects of my creative life. In fact, in the past five minutes, my oldest daughter has come up to my office twice—once to ask for my credit card number (The Mother Bank) for her guitar class, and again to see if she could brainstorm ideas with me for her Human Growth and Development project which isn't due until next month.

Yes, I love my daughter deeply, and I do care about her schoolwork and her guitar class and her volunteer job and her summer plans. But she happens to be home from school due to conferences while I'm *working*, thank you very much, and if she interrupts me again I think I'll scream! (I forgot to tell you about *teen time*, which makes child time seem like a day at the beach.)

For young children, interruptions are often a way to test our devotion. When our attention is elsewhere, they seem to have a burning need to know if we are still available to nurture them. As I said in the chapter on cycles, sometimes the ages of our children just make it plain impossible to capture much creative time at all—and during those times in my own life I almost always gave in to the nurture call.

But I do think that as our children become adolescents and teenagers, it's perfectly acceptable to ask them to respect our creative time. This teaches them that *sometimes their needs must wait*, and personally, I don't want my children heading out into the real world without that particular skill. Now I do make exceptions for extreme bleeding and natural disasters, but they can handle snack selection and sibling strife on their own.

Getting Sidetracked

I want to tell you about an intriguing piece of time-related behavior that began to reveal itself during a number of my interviews. I was fascinated to learn that I wasn't the only creative woman suffering from this particular malaise. I've begun to call it the Sidetracked by Chaos Syndrome, and I have a feeling that it affects a huge portion of the creative mother population. Listen to how Moira Keefe describes it:

My biggest problem is that I'm an anal-compulsive person. I go to other people's homes and see that they're complete slobs—yet totally happy! But in order for me to sit down and work, I have to have things in total order. I have to know that the clothes are clean. This summer, my husband and the kids went away for twelve days. The first day I cleaned, and with the eleven remaining days I wrote my new show. It was great. I didn't have to pick up after anyone. I know there are people who can work in chaos, but I can't.

Christy Cutler expresses similar thoughts:

Organization is the key. I'm compulsive about it. I'm a list maker and a neat-nik. I have to keep things organized physically, and have visual order so that I can un-clutter my mind.

I can't tell you how relieved I was to have my own peculiarities validated—to find out that I wasn't the only woman who not only had to do the breakfast dishes before I could write, but also scour out the dog bowl with a toothbrush and do combat on the cobwebs. I always thought I was creatively mutant, and that truly creative people thrived on mess and disorder with complete disregard for domestic harmony.

Gleefully, I report to you that I'm not so mutant after all, and that many of us find that to enjoy creative time we must first use some of our time to straighten, fix, and clear a clean path. Christy views it as a way to free the mind of clutter—that by first ordering our surroundings we can then welcome the *disorder* of creative thinking.

I take it even one step further, believing that the need to create harmony in our physical surroundings actually mimics the creative process itself. It's almost like a practice session for creativity—or foreplay—to begin trying to make sense of chaos before we actually engage in the creative process. We must be primed to create—on the page, on canvas, on a dance floor, at the piano—and our warm-up is the athlete's equivalent of stretching.

If stopping to match up stray socks before starting your creative work isn't something you'd ever do—rejoice. You're free of the obsessive gene and manage to get your stretching some other way. But if you practice your creativity by ordering your work and living space, go easy on yourself. You're not necessarily wasting time or procrastinating. And remember that it's not necessarily a gender thing—plenty of men practice chaos management, too. My husband could work while the house actually splintered apart over his head, but he reports that a good number of the men at his creative company have supremely organized desks and offices.

I would caution, however, that if you experience a severe degree of the Sidetracked by Chaos Syndrome, to the point that you spend all of your time organizing and none of your time creating, you should probably seek the help of a qualified professional. There's a difference between scrubbing the dog bowl once and scrubbing it all day long.

Procrastination

Procrastination is a dirty word in our culture, conjuring images of laziness, sloth, and moral weakness. We are trained to delve easily into any task, without ambivalence or reservation. We think we should simply begin that project (even our creative work), make that phone call, pick up where we left off last time and get over ourselves already.

But I think that procrastination is really about fear, and that fear is a part of all creative work. If we didn't fear our creative impulses (which can be wild and strange), and if we didn't fear that *this time* we just won't be able to do it, to access it, we wouldn't be experiencing the creative force. Fear goes with the territory, and eventually it works in our favor. Because the biggest fear of all is the one that screams out, *"What if I DON'T create? Then how can I be alive?"* That fear spurs us on and makes us move our stubborn feet across the dance floor and our fingers across the keyboard.

Deadlines

Procrastination rears its ugly head most often when we're working under a deadline, and most creative work does happen with fixed points of beginning and ending. Performances and concerts happen on specific dates, books must be submitted to meet publication schedules, gallery shows have public openings, and poetry readings take place every weekend at the local coffeehouse.

When we're close to being finished, but not quite done, procrastination visits us with a renewed intensity. When we know we have to get started, but the deadline seems distant and removed, procrastination lures us away from our work to more seductive pleasures.

What's to be done? I try to acknowledge the pattern, and think about the fear using familiar analogies from childbirth. If I can't get started, maybe the fear is of not being able to conceive in the first place. If I can't get to the end, perhaps what I'm fearing is what happens when I finally give birth to the creative work and am then left empty again. Use your experiences of motherhood to help lessen the hold of deadline fear. The cycles of creativity are natural and repetitive—not unlike the experience of holding and letting go of our children on a daily basis.

If you're going through a difficult time when procrastination seems to be more powerful than your creative work, ask yourself the following questions:

- Right now, am I afraid of creating or of *not* creating?

- Do I have the support I need to do this work?

- Am I engaging in self-care, proving that I believe in the importance of this creative work?

- Are too many interruptions destroying my creative impulses?

- Is my creative time being absorbed by mother time and child time?

- Do I have enough freedom from physical chaos to create today?

The answers to these questions may provide you with some valuable information about your creative work and about the origins of your procrastination. Just remember that fear feeds us in the end, and that if we're not feeling a certain amount of healthy fear, we may be involved in creative work that ultimately lacks sustenance.

Professional Time

One final piece of the time pie for creative women is the time we need to spend on the business aspect of our work. Depending on our specific projects and creative focus, this may amount to only a few hours a month, or as much as a few hours every day. We may need to tackle correspondence, network, market ourselves, negotiate a contract, make calls, keep our financial records up to date, or purchase new supplies. Whether you're a beginner in your creative field or a seasoned professional, you need to commit time to managing your career.

Few of us enjoy these tasks, and even fewer of us have any formal training in executing them. We say to ourselves, "I'm a dancer! What the heck do I know about marketing?" But when our creative work is also our profession, the business side becomes as important as the creating. If we ignore the business end, we stand to lose credibility, visibility, money, and opportunities. I'm not an expert in this area, but I have learned a few things over the years:

- Do three small things (only three!) a day relating to the business side of your creative work. Make one call, return one e-mail, put a letter in the mail—and you're done for today.

- Realize that business details are really seeds that you plant in the world. They can grow into something lovely, if tended.

- Delegate chores you truly hate: doing your taxes, framing your photographs, typing up notes, etc. You don't have to *do* it all, you just have to make sure it gets done.

- If you're having trouble getting started creatively, spend half an hour on business. You'll then be eager to move on to the fun part.

- Reward yourself for completing boring business tasks. Refer to the chapter on self-care for ideas.

- Be proactive! Your dream depends on it.

In an earlier chapter we discussed the benefits of joining groups and organizations. The author's league I belong to offers all sorts of business support, including contract consultation, legal advice, networking opportunities, newsletters full of professional advice, and a Web site listing upcoming events and freelance work. If you feel "business challenged," research the organizations in your area that may provide support and encouragement.

The bottom line here (listen to that professional lingo!) is realizing that you must commit time to keeping your creative career alive. It won't happen on its own, even if you have an agent, manager, publicist, or secretary. You must be willing to learn what you don't yet know, and use the skills you already possess. Ask questions every time you meet someone else who does what you do, or what you hope to do. Most people are flattered to share what they know.

Professional time is as necessary to your dream as *creative time*. So schedule it on your calendar, roll up your sleeves, and get busy. You will eventually see results for every hour you dedicate—and it's a worthy cause!

To Contemplate

• How did you spend your time yesterday? Did you have mostly mother time? Did you access creative time or professional time? What are your hopes for using your time tomorrow?

• Are you asking for support and practicing self-care so that you can believe in the worth of making time for your creative work?

• What three things would you like to learn about the business/professional side of your creative career? Who can help you learn what you need to know?

Wise Words

"Don't fill all of your time that is unencumbered by children with the shopping, laundry, and domestic chores. It takes discipline to say, 'I'll shop later. I need this time to be creative.' The irony is that you can accomplish a bunch of errands in two hours' time and feel very productive, but feel you are wasting those same hours if they are spent staring at the computer while you think and prepare to write."
—Michele Bograd

"Actually, I think I'm doing a good thing by showing my kids that occasionally I'm selfish. This way they see that I'm a mom who has a creative life separate from them."
—Dee Paddock

"Demand time for yourself. Tell your partner you need chunks of time to be creative—that you can't do it all. Someone else has to cook dinner a couple of times a week. Someone else has to go through the kids' closets and get rid of the clothes that are three sizes too small."
—Moira Keefe

Chapter Nine

The Money Thing

"People who write novels
often live in hovels."

—Anne Lamott
Operating Instructions

Oh, how I wish I didn't have to get into *the money thing*. It's not that I'm sensitive to discussing financial matters. It's just that I'm completely disinterested and always have been. In this particular way, I neatly fit at least one stereotypical view of creative people—I'd rather do just about anything (swim in shark-infested water, for instance, or eat a plate of haggis) than think about money. I'm not proud of this, mind you, and I don't want my daughters to follow in my footsteps. I want them to understand the GNP, make fabulously successful investments, and know how to track and manage their money.

It will help if it turns out that they've inherited that special little gene—you know, the one that makes you thrill at the combination of letters that spell out NASDQ and IPO (are they designers of gym shoes?). My husband has the gene, as does Ruth, his sharp-minded, financial whiz of a mother. My own mother always managed our family's finances, as do my sister and sister-in-law. So you would think that I had a fairly good chance of receiving that gem of a gene, but alas, I simply did not. I think I got thick hair and a highly acute sense of smell instead, but these seem like consolation prizes in comparison.

However, I can't deny the fact that *the money thing* is an important subject to explore, and one that mothers who do creative work need to better understand. The women I interviewed rated the lack of money right up there with *the time thing* as a major life stress. So let's dive in and look at how *the money thing* affects our creative work and our family life.

Cheryl Richardson, in her book *Take Time for Your Life*, devotes a chapter to financial health and has this to say:

> Most of us have never received any basic training in the art of handling money. It seems we go straight from independent, carefree childhood to the fiscal responsibilities of adulthood. Feeling insecure about money, we rarely seek help until we find ourselves in debt, approaching middle age and struggling to save, or coming up short at the end of the month. The way we handle money may be based on the way our parents handled money, and chances are they didn't receive any training either.

I think she's absolutely right. And I think that people in creative careers have an even bigger challenge than "handling" money. We first have to figure out how to *make* money in a culture that places little concrete value on what we do. We have to believe in ourselves enough to ask for fair market compensation, and to be willing to confront the fallacy that we do what we do "out of love."

Making a Living Creating

I don't like putting bumper stickers on my own car, but sometimes I see one that makes me laugh with recognition. A longtime favorite is the one that says, *"Wouldn't it be great if schools had as much money as the military and the army had to hold a bake sale?"* Along those lines, I've often wanted to create my own bumper sticker that asked the question, *"Wouldn't it be great if artists made as much as sports figures and NFL players had to do it for cheap just because they love the game?"*

Every single person I know who works in a creative field has had to endure the ignorant comments from fellow humans about the worth of artistic pursuits. It's not unusual for someone to remark, *"Well, I know people in the arts don't make a lot of money, but that's not why you do it, is it? I'm sure you do it because you love it."* This always leaves me feeling vexed. I never assume that other professional people perform their jobs only because they love them, without thought to compensation.

I remember a time when I was being examined by a doctor I hadn't met before. During the predictable small talk designed to make us all forget that one of us is naked beneath an open-backed gown, I revealed that I was a writer. He told me that he had always wanted to be a writer, too, and that sometimes he thought about leaving medicine for a summer to write a novel he'd begun in college. I kept my mouth shut, but I wanted to say, pointedly, "You know, Doc, that's funny because *I* always wanted to be a high-paid doctor. In fact, I'm thinking about quitting writing and doing a little surgery this summer."

I've met lawyers who tell me essentially the same thing (substitute screenplay for novel): "Maybe I should quit the Bar and take my chances in Hollywood." To which I want to reply,

"Gee, what a good idea! I'm thinking of giving up writing and arguing some cases in front of the Supreme Court. What do you think?"

My friends laugh at these stories, but they actually illustrate an important fact. Most people assume that it's really quite simple to be a writer, actor, dancer, artist, or musician—that all you have to do is quit that pesky day job and *decide* to be creatively successful. These people give little thought to the years and years that it takes to creep toward proficiency in creative fields, much less to the notion of life-long study, sweat, skill, and innate talent.

Oh, and *the money thing*. You rarely hear someone say, "Hey, guess what? I've decided to leave my $200,000 job at that little real estate development company to take up sculpture. I don't have any real training or skill, and I'll lose my stock options, but I think it'll be a blast to live on an eighth of my former salary and have no benefits!"

And then there's my favorite story of the time I was asked to "take a meeting" with the obscenely wealthy executive of a TV cable company. He had an office bigger than my entire house, with panoramic views, white sofas, and a restaurant-quality espresso machine. He wanted someone to ghostwrite a novel for him, based on an idea he'd been mulling over since college. He yammered on about how his L.A. connections would probably result in a movie deal once the book was published, and yadda-yadda-yadda.

When I openly blanched at the meager price that he was willing to pay for this work-for-hire, he became irritated. When I told him my agent would have to negotiate the deal, he became incensed. He told me there were plenty others like me to be found who would work for a "fair" price, and that I had just "said no to the wrong person." I walked out of his office in a very dignified manner, but I had to restrain myself from tossing my cup of espresso on one of his too-white sofas.

To me, this is a prime example of how our culture views the little people who put their creative gifts out into the world—that what we have to offer is somehow less deserving of financial reward than the talents of Napoleonic, espresso-swigging guys who bring televised home shopping channels into our living rooms.

If I sound as though I'm ranting, perhaps I am. But I want desperately to reinforce how hard it is to make a living doing creative work. Very few of us (myself readily included) ever reach the point where our creative projects alone cover our cost of living. Most of us teach, temp, freelance, and do all sorts of unrelated jobs in order to pay our bills. And yes, we *do* love our creative work—we can't imagine doing anything else—but that doesn't mean we should embrace the notion of poverty. Loving one's work doesn't equate to working for free, and I think it's time to let go of that tired old notion.

The next time someone makes an ignorant comment to you about your work, I recommend saying something like this:

> You know, for every Stephen King and Andy Warhol and Julia Roberts out there in the world, there are hundreds of thousands of others like me who are struggling fiercely to make a living from our creative work. We're the ones working in your community theatres, we're teaching art after school at the YMCA. We're writing advertising copy for your business, and we're making costumes for the ballet you're attending this weekend. It's taken years of hard work and dedication for me to get where I am today, and no, you couldn't repeat my efforts just by deciding today to quit your job and do what I do. I have training, skill, and ex-

pertise, not to mention some natural talent. I love what I do, as I'm sure you love your work, and I'd love to be paid what I think I'm worth. If I tell you what I really make from my work, you'll probably tell me I should wake up and find a way to use my skills to a better financial end. If I then tell you that I've done just that and I'm now writing romance novels under a pen name or designing birthday cards for a big card company, you'll tell me that I've "sold out" and polluted my art. And I tell you that if our culture valued the "unpolluted" arts, we'd have drama and music in every school, the National Endowment for the Arts would have a huge, abundant budget to support artists of every kind and at every level, and we'd recognize the value that creative expression could bring to a society plagued by sickening violence, corporate pandering, and an over-inflated attachment to meaningless commercial goods.

Now, if that doesn't stop the cocktail conversation, you might just try producing your tax returns for the past five years. That should do the trick—though you might not be invited back to the party!

Money Bites

Okay, enough from my personal soapbox. Here's what some of our Big Purple Mommies have to say about *the money thing*. You remember Clarice who lives in New York and works as an actress. During our interview I asked her if she ever wished she made the same kind of salary as people who work in Corporate America.

Absolutely! But I wouldn't do a Corporate America job to get it. I'd like to succeed financially in my own field—that's an absolute dream. But my agent gets 10% of what I make, and my ex-husband gets 17% for child support (even though he's doing quite well), and then when you take out taxes, I'm living on 50% of my income. I don't have a lot of clothes. I don't have a car. I don't have good health care. But I'm basically a happy person. I'm a working actor. I'm not a household name, but I'm working in the theatre and I still get to be a mother, that's all I ever wanted.

Keep in mind that Clarice is an incredibly talented woman— that she lights up the stage, and brings a quality experience to every member of the audience, night after night. She has a degree in theatre, several decades of experience, and she's performed in many of our country's largest regional theatres. She has achieved mastery over a difficult craft. When she's not in a production, she does temporary office work and teaches acting. In her mid-forties, she shares her apartment with several roommates and thinks about every dollar she spends.

So tell me. *Is this someone who deserves to not have the basics in life, like adequate health care? What's going on here?*

The Lure of the "Real Job"

Moira Keefe says that her creative work could radically change with just a bit more money every month, and that she often thinks she should just give up and go get a "real job."

Even if I had as little as an extra two hundred dollars a month, I could hire someone to help me with the administrative stuff—send out script packets and help me with bookings—and this could result in new business. When I perform, on a good night I can pack in 150 people and make around $800 dollars. But on a bad night, there can be as few as fifteen people, and I still have to pay rent on the theatre, and pay a technician and box office person. At the end of the month when the bills come in and Spouse and I get into an argument about money, I think maybe I should get a "real" job from about four P.M. until midnight. That way I'd at least miss the after school and bedtime duty!

Though Moira told me she was joking about the four to midnight shift, she says the lure of a "real job" is always out there—like some kind of stable lighthouse in a rough sea. She *wants* to spend her life writing and performing, but making a go of it financially is precarious and frustrating.

I wonder about the origins of the phrase "real job." Who decided that creative work isn't "real," while the work of an accountant or engineer means you're *very* real? How often have you told someone what you do, only to have that person look at you skeptically and ask, "I know, but what do you *really* do?" The implied message here is that unless you can claim large sums of money for your creative work, you aren't *really* doing anything.

Many of us do end up in more traditional jobs, which cover our expenses, and enable us to continue our creative work "on the side." Again, I think our choice of words can wound, relegating our life's passion to a "side" dish rather than the "main course."

And yet, sometimes we can make the main/side arrangement work out beautifully. A friend of mine, a gifted poet and college instructor, recently took a "real" job at an Internet company. She grew tired of trying to string together a living from part-time teaching and writing, and wanted more financial breathing room for her family. Though she went into the job somewhat reluctantly, she's had an amazing rise in her company. She now holds a senior management position and makes an impressive salary. And she's been able to realize a lifelong dream of owning a beautiful horse, which she and her daughters ride every chance they get.

Her choice to work in the "real" world has been agonizing at times, but things are going well for her. She still publishes her poetry and essays in magazines, and keeps her writer identity alive. And if I introduced her to you I'd say, "I'd like you to meet my friend the poet." I definitely *wouldn't* say, "I'd like you to meet my friend who has a 'real' job with an Internet company and does a little poetry on 'the side.' "

Giving people the label of "real" only in accordance with job title and salary is a none-too-subtle form of discrimination. It devalues those of us who work in creative fields, and anyone outside the nine-to-five, regular paycheck lifestyle. The one obvious way we can fight back is by being courageous enough to name ourselves (*I write, I paint, I sing, I design, I speak, I perform, etc.*), and to insist loudly that this is, indeed, our absolutely "real" work in the world.

Partners with "Real" Jobs

Christy Cutler laughed as she explained her financial situation to me:

Well, I make money from my work. But I once figured out that even if I taught dance full time, I'd make a whopping $20,000 a year. Right now I make about $12,000 a year, including workshops. It makes me sad, because I've never wanted to do anything that was lucrative. I wanted to teach dance, do art, write children's books, be a midwife—all areas where you aren't paid very much.

She went on to explain that without her husband's career as an attorney, she wouldn't be able to survive teaching dance.

I feel like a "kept" woman [laughter]. Because my husband has a traditional career and makes good money, I'm allowed to do what I do. It figures into everything else we've been talking about—including how I feel about this creative career. If I were a single mother, I couldn't easily afford to take care of myself doing what I do, much less my children. Or, I'd have to do it in a much different way.

I know what Christy is talking about, because I share a similar situation. Though I have worked almost every year of my marriage and always contributed to our household income, my husband contributes more. His job has a regular paycheck, health benefits, and investment plans. At this point in my life, I couldn't support myself and my children on what I earn as a writer. My husband's hard work makes it possible for me to pursue my dream.

And yet—we mustn't forget an important fact. Women who are home with their children, or are working part-time while raising children, also make it possible for their partners to pursue *their* dreams. Freed from the nine-to-five responsibility of child rearing, many of our partners have the luxury of establishing uninterrupted careers with built-in longevity and earning power. What we sometimes forget is that in addition to whatever work we do in the world, we have the additional and hugely serious job of raising our children.

Recently I received an official-looking form from Social Security that's now being sent annually to Americans reaching the age of forty. If you haven't yet received one—be prepared. It contains your entire earning history, from the very first time you filed a tax return until the present. Mine showed what I earned as a high school lifeguard, a college waitress, a twenty-five-year-old receptionist, and a forty-year-old writer who had sold a children's book series to a major publisher. It showed that I had worked every single year of my life from 1974 until 1999—*except for one year!*

It took me a while to figure out why that one particular year showed the lonely sum of "0." I scanned my memory for a few minutes, staring at the date, and then it came to me. Bingo! That was the year I had a newborn, a two-year-old and a five-year-old, and I didn't have one spare minute to do anything but try to keep all of us alive and fed, day to day. I didn't write, I didn't teach, but I worked harder than I ever had in my entire life.

So, you can imagine my chagrin, when, that same year, my husband and I bought an old house with more room for our growing family and had to apply for a loan. I remember sitting in the tiny cubicle, all three children in tow, milk leaking from my breasts. The serious, business-attired loan officer looked at me over his glasses and said, "Now, let me get this straight, for the records. You, Larry, reported such and such earnings last year, am I right? And you, Coleen, last year you made—*nothing?*"

I think I may have gasped in embarrassment. I know I thought that the entire world heard that word *nothing*—that it reverberated throughout the city. Possibly my newborn even understood what was being implied and doubted her choice in me as her mother! I know I ended up nodding silently, unable to explain to this man that I had been employed *full-time* as a mother, with no time off, no benefits, no pension plan, and no lunches out with colleagues. To have him look at me as though I was somehow a slacker not carrying my weight enrages me all these years later.

If creative work is not seen as "real" work, then the work of mothers is downright invisible. You can't be approved for a home loan by saying that you've been gainfully and successfully employed for fifteen years as a mother. That won't get you an empty box. And yet there have been studies that show that the unpaid work of mothers, if broken down by description and amount of hours and given market value, would be unaffordable for most families. The cost of hiring others to do what mothers do—cooking, cleaning, driving, shopping, child tending, etc. would be astronomical.

Last fall, my neighbor went out of town for a week to visit family. She asked me to fill in for her in our carpool, and I readily agreed. Several days later she delivered a twelve-page document to my door, outlining the various people who would fill in for her during her absence. I was amazed, but not surprised as I read through the itinerary. It would take her husband and eight different friends and neighbors to drive, babysit, and tend to her four children for six days—covering what she normally does by herself every day of the year!

Remember this if you're ever in the unfortunate position of being asked the unforgivable question, "And let's see . . . you make *nothing*?"

Working Smaller

Aisha Zawadi rated money as a bigger challenge than finding time to paint:

To paint is expensive! Acrylic paints are expensive. I don't work in oil, which I'd really like to do. I like the quickness of paint, and since I like to work big so I can do big, expressive movements—the canvas size and amount of paint add up. The minimal size for a small canvas is thirty dollars. A jar of paint—a quart, depending on the quality—can run fifteen to thirty dollars. The brushes can go from two dollars for the cheapest all the way to fifty dollars for a high-quality brush. Art supplies generally go low on the list, after rent, food, clothing, doctors, etc. Sometimes for special occasions people give me gift certificates to the art store. I work on smaller canvasses than I'd like, and sometimes I'll just draw more instead of paint.

I applaud Aisha's resilience in the face of an imperfect situation. But it makes me sad, nonetheless. To accept the fact that we must compromise and make our creative work "smaller" or "less than" we imagined because of financial demands is a bitter pill. Women are good at "making do" and "spinning straw into gold" and all those other tired images, but it doesn't make it right.

And yet, working smaller is a better option than not working at all. Gracie Carr says that she composes songs instead of symphonies because a song can usually be completed in a manageable amount of time, therefore satisfying the creative need for completion.

Being paid for our work is the one thing that allows us to work "big." If you sell a painting, you can afford supplies for the next one. If you sell a book, the advance pays for the time you set aside to write. If you are paid to be in a play, you can do your creative work instead of your office temp job. It's the crux of the matter, really, the catch-22. Without financial return for our creative work, we must either set the work aside completely, or work in very small chunks of time as we earn our money elsewhere. And as mothers, we must balance any time spent creating with the demands of raising our children.

Rags to Riches to . . .

One of the most interesting stories about money and creative work comes from Jahnna Beecham, who has experienced both scarcity and abundance through her writing, and has some advice for us all. Hers is not the classic story of "rags to riches," because it actually chronicles a cycle of creativity and money that goes from rags to riches to rags to . . . who knows?

When Jahnna and her husband began writing children's books, they were married but not yet parents. Because they owned very little, they rented a tiny place that came furnished with all the basics, "including silverware," Jahnna says with a laugh. They lived paycheck-to-paycheck, receiving about three thousand dollars per book. And then in one bizarre and wonderful two-week period, they sold two book series to two major publishers.

"Basically," says Jahnna, "we went from near poverty to the prospect of making one hundred thousand dollars in a year." Hardly believing their own luck, they entered into an intense work period where they had to turn in a 150–200 page book every month of the year, while also doing re-writes on finished books and writing outlines for books yet to come. "It was incredible," she adds, "but all we did was work, and I never got out of my pajamas. The only person I talked to other than my husband was the FedEx guy who came to pick up manuscripts."

Then Jahnna discovered she was pregnant, and life accelerated even more. She and Malcolm, who previously had rented their silverware, now purchased a house, a car, furniture, clothes, a designer crib, and "started buying imported beer instead of the generic-brand beer!" They had a son, then a daughter, wrote more and more books, hired a full-time babysitter, and managed to keep their earnings astoundingly high. But the pressure to manage the cost of their lifestyle was severe, and when both of their book series ended at around the same time, they had no idea what would happen next.

Jahnna describes the next period of their life as "stumbling along, trying to piece together our same income by writing for other authors and ourselves." She also points out that because they chose to live in beautiful but remote places (like Montana and Oregon), they were away from major centers of commerce where they could pursue "real" jobs. "On the high end, these locations have doctors and lawyers, and everyone else works for minimum wage. There's not much in between."

Their worries disappeared for a time when they began to break into the brand-new and flourishing field of writing for the computer world. CD-ROM was new technology and writers could earn substantial amounts of money scripting the stories for kids' computer games. "We took another unbelievable leap," says Jahnna. "We were now making *two hundred thousand dollars a year*, if you can believe it, and we did that for several years. The more we earned, the more we spent. We bought a bigger house in a new location that had a scary monthly mortgage. Our children were in private schools and we took some great vacations. But we never stopped working, and at least twenty-five percent of every day was spent trying to bring in new writing assignments, just to keep up with our expenses."

And if you're following the rhythm of this story, you won't be surprised to learn that the bottom was about to drop once again. As the CD-ROM craze grew more commonplace, writers' salaries fell substantially and opportunities became harder to find. Though she and Malcolm were still writing their own books, the series were smaller with fewer books in each. And they were running into the most common problem of the free-lance lifestyle—waiting for checks to arrive for work that has long been finished and turned in. Their income fell to less than half of previous years, yet their cost of living remained the same.

"It's impossible to budget," Jahnna explains. "You don't really have any idea how much you'll make in a given year, so you don't know how much money to withhold for taxes. And since you're sometimes waiting months to be paid, you end up borrowing money just to survive in the meantime. You know what your monthly expenses are, but you don't have any real idea about your financial picture month-to-month or year-to year. It's not the same as getting a regular check each month for the same amount of money."

In yet another chapter of their story, Jahnna and Malcolm have since sold their home and bought a smaller one with a mortgage 75 percent lower than before. They're taking a hard look at their entire financial picture, saying with chagrin, "How could you sell a total of seven million copies of eighty-two separate books and not be a millionaire?"

Jahnna admits that a lack of money management experience and huge fluctuations of income contributed to their problems, and concedes that most people in creative fields don't ever acquire economic expertise. "Part of the reason," she thinks, "is that as writers and artists and actors you never actually believe that you'll make real money. You don't quite believe it even when it's happening. And you don't get how rare it is to succeed until much, much later. Inside, you always feel like the same people who had to rent a house that came with silverware."

While they are trying to become more savvy now about college funds and retirement accounts, Jahnna says that a certain amount of risk-taking is necessary to the entrepreneurial lifestyle. The highs and lows have been dramatic and stressful, but she says, "We have a wonderful life. We've been able to live the creative dream, and now we're having to learn to be more grounded about money."

Final Words on the Money Thing

Jahnna's story may seem unreal to you, especially if, like me, the thought of ever making several hundred thousand dollars a year in the arts seems about as likely as being set down in the middle of Oz. But even though her saga is extreme, it contains valuable information for all of us. We do have to think about such mundane things as retirement, college for our children, paying taxes, and staying financially healthy. If our children show any inclination toward creative fields, we have a solemn responsibility to educate them in practical matters. I am encouraged to learn that many fine arts college programs now include required courses on "the business of the arts."

I should have been so lucky as to have those particular college credits to my name. I joke with my husband that because we may never be able to retire, we need to begin planning for the "real" jobs of our golden years. He's in favor of being greeters at a big discount chain, though I think we'll be too grumpy to do all that smiling and greeting. My vote is for becoming employees of the National Parks, selling campsite passes and firewood to tourists. You get those nifty uniforms with ranger hats, and I think you get a trailer to live in.

I can just hear my husband saying, "Howdy, folks! Welcome

to God's country. You can park your RV over in campsite sixty-three, and don't forget to stop by and get some firewood from the missus!"

On that note, I think I better call my accountant and get back to work.

And so should you.

To Contemplate

• What connections do you make between the intrinsic value of your creative work and our culture's sense of its worth? How about the value you place on your unpaid work as a mother? In the absence of a paycheck, how do you allow yourself to feel valued?

• Are you paying attention to the business and financial aspects of your creative work? What do you need to do or learn to increase your financial health and expertise?

Wise Words

"I never live up to my means because then I wouldn't be able to save. Don't try to compete with other people around dollar signs."
—Clarice Williams

"I tell people I've already done the world tour of freebies and performing in church basements. I did two or three years of it for free—because I loved the work. Now I'm better with my boundaries, and

the time I have to take away from my family means
something. I'm not adverse to telling an organiza-
tion that they need to pay my going rate or I won't
be able to come. I value my work, and I place a
value on the time I have to take from my family."
—Dee Paddock

"I think that when you have to make money, there
are times when you take jobs that you're not the
perfect person for, and things don't turn out so
great. I'm learning to say no to the jobs that don't
turn me on, but still—you have to pay the rent."
—Wendi Schneider

"I think I probably seem vague about prices for my
work, and some collectors get annoyed. But I don't
think about money. It seems like $30.00 and
$300.00 are about the same—not much money.
$3,000.00 is better. Everything seems to cost a
lot. When you estimate the cost of anything, add
another zero to the end."
—Lady McCrady

Chapter Ten

Where We Create

> "Creating a harmonious, meaningful
> environment in space and time helps
> you to become personally creative."
>
> —Mihaly Csikszentmihalyi
> *Creativity*

We cannot begin our creative work in earnest until we are able to name ourselves by what we do. Until we can walk into a party and say, after several strong drinks and much throat clearing, "I am a writer. I write things. That is what I do—I write!" Or whatever *you* do. Fill in the blank. But until you can give a name to your passion, you won't seriously think you need, or merit, your own workspace. And until you have a space that is yours, you can't spread out, make a mess, make mistakes, daydream, twiddle your thoughts, and become the creative person you are meant to be.

Of course, if you're an actor or dancer, you may argue that you do your creative work in many places—that the world is your workspace. But what do you do when you get home? I would still say that you need at least a corner, somewhere, where you can store your notes, your books, your calendar, your candle, the reminders of your ongoing creativity.

Sometimes the journey to claiming a personal, creative workspace is a long one. It certainly was for me. To this end, I offer you a brief tour of my varied and successive workspaces, in the hopes that it will encourage you to keep clamoring and searching for that perfect place in which to do your creative work.

A Garage, An Attic, Two Bedrooms, and Pay Dirt!

After I married for a second time and finally broke through the dark abyss and began to call myself a writer (in no small part due to the urgings and support of Larry), I experienced the true joy of having my first legitimate workspace. Who can fully describe the secret thrill of one's very own filing cabinet—that gleaming, metallic, four-drawer hunk of beauty and secrecy? Larry and I shared an office, which was in reality a long, narrow, cold room that had once been the garage of our tiny bungalow. We furnished it with a makeshift desk made of a hollow-frame door resting on two sawhorses. We had a bulky, not-so-reliable first-generation computer and printer, and a spare kitchen chair on which to sit.

This was a step in the right direction toward having my own space, though sharing an office with my husband meant I shared an office with his clutter. And I'm talking *clutter*. Piles of it. Newspaper clippings, magazines, manuscript pages, office supplies scattered everywhere, trash that always seemed to miss the wastebasket. And being a person who needs visual harmony in order to feel peaceful enough to work, this arrangement had its drawbacks. Larry felt forced to endure my compulsive standards of neatness and I felt undone by his tolerance for chaos. And then, of course, we had to negotiate our schedules so that we could each have time in the workspace, away from the penetrating personality of the other.

Did I mention the fact that this cave-like room was also by default the guestroom? The ancient twin bed shoved against the wall and covered with Larry's fuzzy orange spread from his bachelor days held the occasional out-of-town guest, and more often, the parent who most needed a night of not getting up with a crying baby. All in all, our "office" was functional, but served too many other purposes to truly be a haven for creative work.

But that was all about to change, anyway. When we were surprised with the advent of a third child, we realized we would have to convert our wacky office into the new baby's room and forfeit the coveted space altogether. Our other two daughters were already sharing a bedroom and we needed the tiny family room for the growing collection of toys, books, puzzles, and child paraphernalia. But after measuring our own bedroom and realizing that our writing desk wouldn't fit, we knew it was time to take a deep breath and buy a bigger house.

Which we did—an old, rambling, falling apart, almost charming house in a wonderful neighborhood of other old houses and even older trees. It had room for our family and— drum roll, please—an attic office big enough for Larry and I to each have our *own desks*! Yes, we would still have to share the room, but this time I could have my own, impeccably neat desk and Larry could blithely enjoy his stacks and piles and mounds. This arrangement worked well, except for the fact that the attic was unbearably cold in the winter and hot in the summer and the nearest bathroom was one flight down. We couldn't afford to do much toward solving these problems other than investing in space heaters, electric fans, and trying to go easy on the coffee.

But the view from those tiny dormer windows—*oh, my God,*

the view!—was enough to make us forget our lack of creature comforts. We watched, in turn, the tops of trees go from bud to blossom, to full green bounty, then back to yellow and gold splendor, and finally to iced bare branches. We toiled in a virtual tree house and both managed to accomplish a significant amount of our creative work. I wrote several plays during that time which remain personally meaningful, and capture the time in my life when I was deeply entrenched in mothering three very young girls.

Of course, one mustn't forget that one of the chief charms of an attic office is that the sounds of children's voices don't penetrate from below, and that to reach a parent, an enterprising child must climb many flights of steep stairs to reach the place where, quite possibly, the ghosts of cats and old ladies who once inhabited the house can be heard screeching from the cobwebby closet!

After nearly five years of this happy arrangement, we naively sold our beloved house and moved to the Midwest, where I had accepted what I hoped to be a fulfilling creative opportunity in the form of a "real" job at a major theatre. My husband was ready for a break from teaching college English, and I felt it was my turn to be the main breadwinner. Larry would be the parent at home, and work on a book project.

In our rented house in this unfamiliar terrain, my husband claimed a tiny sun porch for his desk and computer and I agreed to a corner of our upstairs bedroom. This was based on the fact that since I would be having a "real" job, at a "real" theatre, where I would be allocated a "real" desk and computer and supplies in a "real" office, it was only fair that Larry have the home office.

This was to be a particularly anguish-filled time in my life, as both the job and move across country turned out to be unsuccessful. Neither desk—at home or at work—could save me from a bleak period of depression. During that year I wrote dozens of heartbroken letters to family and friends, and strangely, what I still consider to be the best play I've ever written. As icicles formed like stalagmites over my bedroom window, I took my bruised writer's soul back to the 1930's, to an American colony in the steamy jungles of Brazil, where my characters were as homesick and displaced as I.

After a grateful move back home to the West, we found temporary housing on a former Air Force base that was in the process of being converted to commercial development. We rented one side of what was once a row of fashionable Officer's duplexes, and my office, once again, was in a corner of the bedroom. My husband took over what should have been the dining room, because by now, our school-aged children needed access to his faster computer for schoolwork and research, and we rarely had use for a formal dining room.

The difference this time is that I was in the place where I knew I belonged, and my view out the window was a breathtaking expanse of the Rocky Mountains. In a rush of starting-over energy and financial desperation, I reinvented myself from a playwright to a children's book author, and tried not to think about the long succession of uniformed men and domesticated wives who had occupied our military issue bedroom/office before us!

During this faux military period, I took to calling my husband Colonel and he called me "The Missus." We did a lot of saluting, and took to telling our girls that they needed to be in bed by 2100 hours—whatever that meant!

After a strange but very healing time on the base, we bought the house we now live in. This part Victorian, part contemporary add-on has its share of problems and imperfections, but what makes it the perfect place is that for the first time in my life, I HAVE MY OWN OFFICE! My very own space shared with no one but the family dog who likes to lie at my feet and look faintly bored while I write. And guess where my husband does *his* work? IN HIS OWN OFFICE! Yes, it's true. We managed to find a house with two home offices and enough other rooms for a family of five to eat, sleep, play, and dream.

Every day I count myself truly blessed to have this sunny place in which to do my creative work. Though fairly small, it features a tiny balcony with a view of the garden and enough room for my desk, books, and of course, that beloved filing cabinet. Here, I'm able to leave my work out and know that when I come back it will still be where I left it. Here, I can retreat from family life and revel in the other half of my identity. Here, I write books, make cards, take notes, make plans, call friends, and sometimes just sit in absolute, glorious silence.

In a pinch I'll let my daughters use my computer, but they have to ask permission and they know I'll be really cranky if they mess with my stuff. They know to respect my space, the way I've always respected theirs. I don't enter their rooms without knocking, I don't read their private writing, and I definitely DON'T MESS WITH THEIR STUFF. In the dense, sticky web of family life, it's the least we can ask of each other.

So, as you can see, it took me a decade to claim the kind of creative space I always wanted. But it was worth the wait. I don't think it's a coincidence that finding the space has allowed me to enter more fully into a period of intense and satisfying creative work. I think it's another old notion that creative people are so obsessed with their internal landscape that they can create anywhere, with little regard to the sensory aspects of their surroundings. It's just not true.

The women I interviewed are extremely particular about

where they create—from the play of light, to the view, to the sounds that come in, to the smell of the room, and the objects that surround them. Not all of them are happy with where they work, which means that the journey toward a more perfect space is still in progress.

Space Bites

Lady McCrady seems to have especially good luck finding workspaces that inspire her painting:

I've always found good, large spaces that seemed to have a bluey-white atmosphere of light to work in. I painted in an older artist's studio on a tidal marsh for a few years. Recently, we built a huge studio with all the money we had, so I can work there from now on.

Wendi, who moves back and forth from painting to her online antiques business, has two different spaces for her work:

I have two workspaces in my home. One is my office, which is in a converted bedroom. It's filled with antiques, and lots of photo props and things that I like to look at. That's where my computer is, and I have a big armchair. And then for painting and shooting, I use the sunroom. It's a great hangout room with lots of light, and it's used more by the whole family.

Though Christy Cutler teaches dance in a large, sun-filled studio with lots of mirrors and a sound system, she does her lesson plans and notes on a computer in her home:

We have two computers in our house, and I use the one that no one else likes, which is downstairs. There I have all of the children's literature that I teach from, as well as a card index I've been building over the years containing ideas for teaching dance. That's where I create my overall and specific lesson plans.

Aisha Zawadi is flexible, using various areas to do her painting, depending on the light and the size of her painting:

I might set a canvas on my kitchen table or on a shelf in my bedroom. During summer or holidays, I might use the art studio at the school where I teach. And I can draw just about anywhere at all—that's portable!

And Moira Keefe, who is still waiting to claim the perfect space, has little good to say about her current situation and tells us in her trademark, straightforward way:

I work in a cramped little dungeon I refer to as my "hell hole." It's a space off the bedroom, and I have this picky husband who tells me he can hear me typing! Not my ideal space, which would be a separate garage turned into an office. We have a guestroom, but we have so many guests that I can't use it as an office. Now, where I work is also where we store all the things I can't get rid of—family photos, kid's art work, old report cards. I have the one crappy room in the house!

Seven Ideas about Space

As you can see, creative women work in all kinds of spaces, and have strong feelings about what does and doesn't nurture their creativity. From a corner of the basement to the kitchen counter, to a spare bedroom turned sanctuary, we claim what we can—sinking a flag of ownership in the sand like our sturdy pioneer grandmothers. I think it's fair to say that Moira is pretty unhappy with her current space while Lady and I may have just achieved our true dream of studios. Together they represent both ends of the space spectrum and give us an insightful perspective for comparison.

Keep in mind that what makes a space "perfect" is a highly individual thing—you might step into my office and have an intuitive, but strong "hit" that the space wouldn't nurture your creativity. The color of the walls might make you sleepy, or the overflowing bookcases could overwhelm your minimalist eye. And I could walk into your lovely space and know within a few minutes that the traffic sounds from the street outside would distract me, even though they don't bother you a bit.

The following ideas are meant only to inspire you to believe that you deserve a space for your creative work, and that the space you inhabit should reflect the unique quality of who you are, and what you create.

1. **You deserve a space that's relegated only to your creative work.** Whether it's a card table set up in a quiet corner of the dining room, or a brand new studio, your creative dreams can't flourish until you claim a space.

2. **Ideally, the space should allow you to separate from your mother identity.** The farther away you can be from major household appliances, the playroom, or the nursery, the better able you'll be to access your creative identity. Try not to let the "stuff" of family life trickle into your space. If you can keep toys and crayons and muddy shoes out of your area, you'll be able to focus more effectively on your creative work.

3. **Fill your claimed space with reminders of your creative work.** Put up a bulletin board on the wall and cover it with photos, cards, notes, and programs—anything that reminds you of your creative identity. Find a completely separate place for school lunch menus, carpool schedules, coupons (that's what refrigerators are for!), and other "mother" stuff.

4. **Make sure you have the kind of light you like.** Whether you need natural light for your artwork, or a good desk lamp for writing, don't just sit there in the dark! Inadequate lighting can definitely affect your energy, focus, and state of mind. If your space lacks light, can you move your table across the room? Can you remove heavy shades or drapery from existing windows? Can you purchase inexpensive lamps to lighten things up? If you have money to spare, can you add a sky light to your space? What would it take to "let the sun shine in"?

5. **Use color to enhance your creativity.** One solution to a dim space is painting it a warm, vivid color. Don't underestimate what a gallon of paint from the hardware store can do for the visual aesthetic of your space. A carefully chosen color can make you feel restful, inspired, energized, or thoughtful. Spend some time researching colors you like and remember to try a small sample before you paint the entire space. If you're currently sharing space in another room of your house, consider painting even one wall, to define the space as yours. When I painted my office a deep, relaxing green instead of the previous peachy-white, I felt immediately more at home in my space.

6. **Think about sound.** Can you work with a steady noise level, or do you need absolute quiet? Does the noise from other places in your home soothe or distract you? Can you

hear street sounds from where you work? Do you like to listen to music while you work and if so, do you have access to a tape or CD player? The solutions to sound problems can be as simple as hanging a quilt on the wall to muffle the sounds of pipes, putting up a simple wooden screen around your area—or as complex as new insulation or double-paned windows.

7. **Believe in the inspirational power of special objects.** Do you have two or three objects in your space that speak to your unique creative energy? Familiar items with personal meaning—candles, stones, carvings, small fountains, a favorite plant, a certain mug for tea—stimulate our senses and help us put a tangible frame around our creative spirit. I know one woman who can only begin her writing if a certain blanket is spread over her lap, and another who ends every work session by fingering a small set of chimes. Give in to the seemingly frivolous need for the security of favorite objects around you—it's the trademark of a creative person.

The "Other" Perfect Space

Besides our own claimed space in which to work, there is a second kind of space to consider as we pursue our creative careers—the actual, physical place where we reside. Do you feel "at home" when you think about the town or city you live in? Does the geography of your location inspire you creatively? Do you have access to other creative people and institutions?

In his book *Creativity: Flow and the Psychology of Discovery and Invention*, Mihaly Csikszentmihalyi explains that historically, creative people have always flocked to the "great centers of learning and commerce" where they could "leave their mark on the culture." This migration of artists also had to do with which communities could finance a creative project—which king or pope had the means to commission a cathedral or palace or twelve panel fresco.

Csikszentmihalyi contends that:

> Certain environments have a greater density of interaction and provide more excitement and a greater effervescence of ideas; therefore, they prompt the person who is already inclined to break away from conventions to experiment with novelty more readily than if he or she had stayed in a more conservative, more repressive setting.

Of course not all of us have the luxury or flexibility to live in Paris, Milan, or New York, where we might have better access to the particular realm of our creative focus. Many of us have made decisions about where we live based on jobs, schools, and the needs of our families, rather than the proximity to "centers of learning and commerce." And truthfully, when we're in the flush of raising our children, experimenting with novelty seems to take a backseat (at least temporarily) to visits to the pediatrician and going to the library to help research the life cycle of jelly fish.

Still, many of us are undoubtedly living in places that bring us only minimal inspiration. Maria Katzenbach hopes to move from the West to her beloved Martha's Vineyard when her son is done with his schooling. There, near the ocean, she feels most connected to her essential spirit. Wendi Schneider dearly misses the cultural stimulation and architectural beauty of New York City, and Moira Keefe, as we know, loathes the suburbs of southern California and longs for the majesty and privacy of Montana and Colorado. When I lived briefly in the Midwest, I couldn't bear the overcast days, the humidity and overhanging greenery—couldn't wait to be back in the West with dry air and the open expanse of deep blue sky. Sometimes where we live isn't the most convenient place for truly thriving in our creative work. As a writer, my career could potentially be different if I lived in the publishing mecca of New York—and yet with a family of five, our lifestyle there would be questionable. An actress who wants to star in Hollywood films may realize that she's at a disadvantage living in North Dakota—and yet have a fervent wish that her child grow up with her hometown cousins instead of in Los Angeles. Artists all over the globe dream of that proverbial garret on the Left Bank—and yet wonder how they would afford their daily baguette, much less canvas and paint.

So much of where we end up has to do with luck, chance, circumstance, and compromise. While it's nice to dream, it isn't particularly helpful to remind ourselves daily that we'd rather be somewhere else if there's little chance we're making a move anytime soon. Unresolved longing can drain our energy and put a negative spin on our creative work. The compromise (that word again) that works for many is making certain to set aside time and resources to visit those longed for places as often as possible. Get to the beach, go to the city, return to the farm—whatever it takes to restore your spirit.

But I also believe that being truly miserable in your soul over where you are living is a slow and painful kind of death that warrants some serious consideration. Sometimes pulling up damaged roots and moving on is the most positive and healthy plan of action. Very little in life is truly irrevocable—I found this out through my own botched move across country. If the notion of a certain place pulls at you so utterly that you can't be creative and can't imagine your family being happy until you get there, then by all means *go*—Get Out of Dodge! Life is short and the world is big.

The Possible Perils of Working at Home

I couldn't live with myself if I left this discussion of place without stopping to talk about the perils of having a creative workspace in your home. Maybe *peril* is too harsh a word, but there are a few things to be aware of once you finally have that perfect space:

1. **The laundry may call out to you in a truly annoying voice.** The scenario goes like this: the children are in school or napping and you're working happily and productively in your perfect space. Until, that is, you go into the kitchen to get a cup of coffee. On the way to the kitchen you step over dirty socks, discarded sweatshirts, and wet towels, and you feel slovenly for letting things pile up, so you decide to just do a quick load of laundry. After all, the washing machine is just a few steps away and it might save time later. You put in the laundry and go back to your work, only to realize that you can't remember where you were or what you were thinking. The solution: just ignore that annoying "wash me" voice. Pick a time outside your creativity time to do domestic chores. The dirty socks will always be there, that moment of inspiration won't.

2. **The phone will ring and you'll think it's your child bleeding profusely from a bizarre playground accident, but it's only some guy trying to sell you aluminum siding.** Most mothers feel the need to be "reachable" while they're working, in case our children or the school tries to call. We lunge at the

phone, spilling paint and erasing files along the way. There is actually little reason for this panic, with all the various technological tools available to us. We can utilize beepers, call waiting, call answering, caller identification and all those other little toys to screen out the calls we don't want and get the messages we need. If you're adverse to these options, for financial or moral reasons, simply ignore the ringing phone and check your messages at regular intervals. Just don't let the need to be "reachable" eat up all of your valuable creative time. And be firm about telling your friends and family that you don't have time to "chat" while you're working and you'll call back later.

3. **At some point, working and living in the same place may make you so restless that you'd accept a lunch date with your ex-spouse, ex-boss, ex–best friend, or ex-drycleaner.** The isolation can get to you. Leave your house and get out into the world. Lunch dates are the perfect solution, as is taking a walk to get a cup of coffee, mail a letter, or run a quick errand. The goal is to at least rub elbows with humanity, if not sit down with it and eat a meal. Just don't make the mistake of going into shops and spending money as a way of relieving your cabin fever—you'll feel momentarily enriched and much poorer later on. Warning: if you spend the entire day in your home, working, creating, and taking care of children, and you never get out, you will go bananas by the end of the day. You will want to fling open the door at dusk and disappear forever. So, go fly, when you can.

4. **Eventually you will need to change your clothes and wear something other than your pajama top and sweatpants.** I know, I know—not having to worry about your

wardrobe is one of the true joys of working at home. As is not showering, not worrying about your cuticles, and not noticing if you smell only a tiny bit better than your dog. But extended periods of "letting yourself go" can have an impact on your self-esteem and your relationships. Wash that hair! Dig into your closet for those things called shirts and pants and lace-up shoes. Do it before one of your children say, "Hey, Mommy, did you know that Johnny's mom works in an office where she has to wear real clothes?"

5. **You will have to throw yourself a one-woman holiday office party.** You don't have a boss. You don't have co-workers. You don't even have a water cooler or a co-ed rest-room. During the holidays, you'll have to pick a day for your party, go into your office, call your partner and say you'll be home late. Open a bottle, have a few swigs, make a pass at yourself, give yourself a joke gift from Secret Santa and call it a day. On your birthday, you'll have to send yourself a card that says *From all of us at the office, many happy returns of the day.* This can be difficult and lonely at times, I admit. But the good news is that you can also give yourself a raise and pro-motion at whim, get the best performance review ever written, and take the day off whenever you darn feel like it. Sometimes when I'm feeling a tad blue, I'll call up a friend of mine who also works at home. He'll listen to me complain for a few minutes and then say, *"Listen, pal, I have to go. I'm taking the ENTIRE staff out to lunch today."*

Final Words

Finding the best possible workspace can be a long journey. Knowing if you're living in the most appropriate geographical location for your creative soul can be a difficult learning curve. Working alone from a home-based space can sometimes make you feel lonely or isolated from humanity. But it's important to remind ourselves that we are privileged to be among those who are actively pursuing our creative dreams—that we are lucky enough and strong enough to acknowledge our gifts and be willing to juggle the demands of our family and the world at large to pursue our soul's work.

Don't forget to keep asking yourself the important questions: *Do I believe today that my creative work is important? Do I have the circle of support that allows me to make time for my work? And do I believe that I deserve a dedicated space in which I can explore my most passionate projects?*

I hope your answers are loudly affirmative.

To Contemplate

- Have you claimed a space for your creative work? If so, does it meet your practical and aesthetic needs? If not, what would it take to improve the space? If you don't yet have a space, do you believe in the importance of your creative work? Do you have the support you need to pursue the journey of claiming a workspace?

Wise Words

"I'm privileged to have an office away from home. It's a totally protected space. The other space is in my home, where I go in the middle of the night or before anyone else rises. There I can reconnect

*with what's what it's like to be in a timeless space
with just my material."*
—Michele Bograd

*"One of the things we don't do in our culture is let
our children into the real struggles of professional
adult life in a salutatory, inspiring way that they can
make good use of. We just hide it all. And that's
one thing about doing your work in your home—your
kids see more of that. They see when you get the
rejection letter, when you have a deadline, when
you're stuck—and see you carry on, no matter
what."*
—Maria Katzenbach

*"My space is an office connected to our bedroom. I
tend to work with lots of piles. I know what's in
them and I take time to organize them. I tend to
think if I sit down to a clean desk my life is in order.
But that's an illusion. If you want to get work done,
you have to work amidst the mess."*
—Dee Paddock

Chapter Eleven

The Big Picture

"Women who become mothers find that
it is often in the crucible of that
experience, in what is in so many ways a
sacrifice of self, that she touches
her deepest experiences of the female self
and wrestles with an angel that
at once wounds and blesses her."

—Naomi Ruth Lowinsky, Ph.D.
Stories From the Motherline

As we end this journey together, I bring you the best piece of news of all. I've saved it for last—a final treat to sustain you. And this is it:

Sometimes, once in a while, all of the elements of our complicated lives come together to produce a stunning chance for creative growth. In the midst of mothering our children and faithfully following the threads of a creative passion, we suddenly find we have the support, the money, the time, and even the energy we need to answer the knock of opportunity. It's happened to me enough over the years so that I believe vehemently in the surprising, serendipitous, and totally unpredictable nature of a larger, collective spirit of creativity operating in the universe.

I promised in the opening chapter that I would tell you the sequel to the Big Purple Mommy story, and here it is.

Going to Montana

Remember that at the time my daughter drew the original Big Purple Mommy, I was in a bleak, mid-winter depression. My mother identity had completely consumed my identity as a writer and I felt sure that the balance would remain cruelly uneven for years to come. I was trying to complete a play in time to submit to a new play festival, but lacked both the energy and confidence to finish. I undermined myself daily, thinking grim thoughts like, *You're no good anyway, this play is weak, the children all have colds, and the world doesn't really need one more wanna-be playwright.*

But somehow, I plodded though the negativity and fear and managed to write a pretty good play, despite the weather and the many runny noses I was responsible for wiping. I put the play in an envelope, addressed it to an enigmatic place in Montana called The Gathering at Bigfork, and dropped it off at the post office. Then I drove home laughing at the thought of gathering anywhere with anyone, outside of my own toy-strewn castle/prison.

And of course, the moral of the story is twofold: be careful what you wish for and know that opportunity never looks quite the way you think it will. After several months of not hearing anything official from the directors of the festival, I resigned myself to not making the cut and turned my attention to other things. Luckily, motherhood keeps you busy enough that you mostly don't have time to dwell indefinitely on the pain of not being chosen. The wounds hurt and you think, *See, told you I wasn't good enough*, but by necessity they heal over fairly quickly.

But one evening in late spring, my husband and I returned home from a rained-out baseball game to a message the babysitter had scrawled about calling some woman with a strange name in Montana about coming to a play festival. I stared at the slip of paper, not making sense of it. I knew the festival was scheduled to begin in less than a week and that the selection of plays had been made months ago.

So I returned the call and was soon talking to a warm and vivacious woman named Jahnna (yes, our very own Jahnna Beecham) who had a long and complicated story to tell me. It seems that one of her selected playwrights had to drop out of the festival, and by sheer coincidence she just that very day happened to find my unopened script stuck underneath her daughter's car seat, where it had mysteriously stayed buried for several months. In short, she loved my play and could I possibly come to Montana for two weeks to rehearse the script for a staged reading with professional actors and directors?

I said *yes!*—breathlessly, excitedly—not thinking about how I would manage to be gone from my home and children for two weeks. My husband and I had done the impossible and escaped for several weekends away together, but I hadn't been on an extended trip alone in years. I hung up the phone, elated for a few moments, until the despondency set in. How could I manage it? Who would take over my various and complicated duties with the children? Could I really go off by myself and assume my creative identity fully and completely and not look like I was coming out of mothballs? Could I be the wild woman in purple that my daughter had drawn?

It turns out that managing the logistics of the trip was actually far easier than dealing with my fear and insecurity. My husband and a rotating roster of babysitters could certainly handle the childcare considerations, and the trip was essentially a cost-free endeavor. So I had the time and money and support aspects in place, and all I needed was to practice enough self-care to be able to pack my bags, get on the airplane and take the plunge into my creative self.

Thankfully, I was able rise to the occasion, after an agonizing week of making arrangements and attending to domestic details. On a rainy May morning I took deep breaths and said a tearful goodbye to my children. Then I headed west to be a playwright and to experience an absolutely magical time of immersing myself in my work, in a sweet little town at the foot of Glacier National Park, with some of the most incredible people I've ever met. I lost myself in rehearsals and rewrites during the day, then lost myself in conversation and hilarity at the local cowboy bar at night. I sat alone by the lake with a cup of coffee, wandered through the boutiques on Main Street, wrote in my journal, slept and showered in complete privacy, ate slowly and thoughtfully with interesting companions, and sometimes got teary-eyed thinking about my husband and children at home.

The reading of my play was a triumphant personal success, as was meeting Jahnna and her family and beginning what still remains a dear and important friendship. Jahnna and I relate as mothers and writers and as women who must constantly overcome nagging and irrational fears. Over the years we've established a pattern of calling to warn each other every time we read a bizarre or frightening story involving children, natural disasters, and freak accidents. We play Danger Ranger for each other, and not just anyone can fill that role in one's life! (She calls with an article that warns me to point my feet in order to soften the impact of the water, if ever I must suddenly jump off of a bridge. I call and tell her not to let her children play in the trunks of cars because of a tragedy in my hometown involving a game of hide-and-go-seek.)

That one simple but courageous act of sending off a script and putting my work out into the world produced unforeseen changes in my life and career. Jahnna has been the connective force for other creative projects that have come my way, and more importantly, by going to Montana I learned the biggest lesson of living the creative life. Unless you remain true to your creative calling and commit to planting small seeds every day, nothing can grow. If you don't send the script, despite runny noses and winter blues, no one will read it. If you don't sing your songs, even though you're running after a toddler or nursing a baby, no one will ever hear you. If you don't take the leap of faith and sometimes travel away from your children, and toward your creative identity, part of your soul will stay malnourished.

The journey you take doesn't have to be a literal one. You don't have to go to Montana to connect with your creative soul and you don't have to leave your children if it's something you can't do. But you do have to take advantage of the rare times when you have the necessary support, money, time, and energy and travel to the place in your creative work that nourishes you completely.

Making a Career of Letting Go

The words "making a career" and "letting go" may seem contradictory in nature, because we tend to think that having a career means trying to assert control, trying to manipulate events and outcomes, and above all, trying to *work* things to our advantage at all times.

It's funny, but I've come to believe that raising children and having a creative career are about something completely opposite—about letting go. Every day, as mothers and creators, we end up relinquishing control and realizing that bigger forces are at work in the outcomes of our children's lives and our work. We can try to do everything "by the book" regarding our children—every positive thing we can think of, or dream of, to influence a positive future. We can feed them healthy foods, take them to the dentist, get them immunized, make sure they get plenty of rest—only to have them fall ill nonetheless. We can send them to good schools and expose them to pre-approved books and culture and religion and our own sturdy values—and yet watch them develop their own code of behavior and morality. We can love them and protect them and nurture them with every cell of our being—and know that they will have to confront their own demons and darkness and sometimes feel alone and unloved.

The same is true in the opposite vein. We may stumble while we carry them and make little and even big mistakes—only to watch them thrive in spite of us. We may be unable to give them the material goods we might covet or the advantages we think are required—only to realize that all they really need is our limitless love. We may berate ourselves for our faults and shortcomings—only to see our children emulate the very best we have inside.

And the same sort of mercurial force is at work in our creative careers. We may think we can make a five-year plan to publish that book or finish that symphony—only to have it take ten years or twenty. We may produce the best thing we've produced by far—only to have it go unrecognized by the world. We may knock on every door and grab at every morsel of a possible opportunity—only to be met with frustration and an empty plate.

And . . . we may send out a script that gets lost under a car seat, but gets magically found. We may answer the phone on a regular day and have a voice on the other end tell us that our poem, play, sculpture, concerto, or workshop is exactly what's needed and where in the world have we been hiding. We may jot down a note to call a certain organization that we heard mentioned at a party, make that one little call, and six months later get a grant or a fellowship or delightful little stipend.

It's all about relinquishing the belief that we're steering the ship. It's about doing everything we can possibly do, and then letting go—over and over, day after day. To our creative career we bring all the lessons we learn from motherhood about patience, endurance, intuition, stubborn commitment, and purely blind faith. To motherhood we bring all the lessons we learn from our creative work—passion, spontaneity, playfulness, flow, and *yes!*—stubborn commitment, and purely blind faith.

I'm starting to see, as I hope you are too, that what we hold in our two separate hands isn't so separate after all. We couldn't be the mothers we are to our children without the creative work that claims us. And we likely wouldn't be the unique, enraptured creative women that we are without the glorious fact of being mothers.

Coming to this realization helps me to hold a very valuable thing in mind—that my children (The Little Purple People) are the beneficiaries of my lessons in letting go. By watching me repeatedly struggle with relinquishing control instead of clinging fiercely to it, they see another way to be in the world.

I want to tell you one final story from my mother life, about getting to that longed for, metaphorical state of Montana—or Nirvana or Narnia or Oz—or wherever you imagine true bliss to be. Only in this case, we're in Florida, and rather than me longing for creative fulfillment, my middle daughter is longing for dolphins.

Spotting Dolphins

It was spring break and we were visiting my mother-in-law. Overdosed on sun, we decided to make our dolphin-crazed daughters happy and do one of those predictable, faintly cheesy tourist things—a two-hour dolphin sighting cruise, complete with a certified marine biologist on board to explain the world of sea mammals to the uninitiated and sunburned passengers.

The morning was hot and still as we boarded our craft bobbing gently in the shallow bay off the Gulf of Mexico. The fact that the boat featured Christmas lights, half-dead potted palm trees, and a full bar should have tipped us off right away. But we gamely found a vacant patio table with plastic chairs on the uncovered top deck and readied our binoculars and camera. Our resident biologist, a handsome and suntanned young man with a microphone, talked us through Dolphin Sighting 101 while a line formed at the bar for Cokes and potato chips.

My ten-year-old daughter, a nature enthusiast, was beside herself with excitement—she'd been waiting *forever* to spot dolphins outside of captivity. I think she envisioned the kind of flying and leaping thing that you pay even more for at Sea World, but she was soon to learn a hard lesson about the cost of purchased bliss. Our boat lurched along at about five miles an hour, staying just inside a bay that was surrounded by million-dollar homes, protected by man-made sea walls, and fronted with tennis courts and swimming pools.

"Do dolphins like it here?" my daughter asked. "So close to these houses?"

I recalled the old television show *Flipper*, which had captivated me as a child. Flipper was a dolphin who *loved* humans, and lived to perform for them, communicate with them, and sometimes even intervene positively in their affairs. Flipper probably wouldn't have minded the ugly mansions, but then Flipper was a certain kind of dolphin, after all. A Hollywood dolphin. I told my daughter to ask our biologist. He told her not to worry, that he had a perfect record going—thirteen sightings in the past thirteen cruises.

This restored her spirits and she trained her eyes patiently on the water, watching for the slip of dorsal fin above the surface. I couldn't take my eyes off the monstrous houses with their sleek boats docked beside them. I thought that if I were a dolphin I'd swim as far away as possible from the houses and the boats leaking fuel into the bay and the gaping tourists. I'd swim deep into the gulf, away from video cameras and guides who blew loud whistles at every sighting of my gentle species.

It was getting hotter and hotter on our pleasure boat and we'd spent at least ten dollars on soft drinks. My mother-in-law was fast asleep in her chair, her head bobbing on her chest in rhythm with the miniscule waves. Oh, how I longed for a school of dolphins to suddenly appear right beside our boat, to dance for my daughter so she could partake in their beauty and mystery and go home with a perfect vacation memory.

But it wasn't to be. Our cruise broke the perfect thirteen record and all of us were awarded rain checks at the end of the long and mostly boring ride. My daughter tried valiantly to be cheerful, telling her grandmother that at least she got to go out on a boat, which was something we couldn't do in our landlocked home in the West. And the five or six refills of soda hadn't been so bad, either. She took a few pictures of the silly boat and wondered all the way home why the thirteen excursions before ours had all enjoyed the pleasure of dolphins and ours had come up dry. I could offer little reason or comfort for these unfortunate odds.

On the last morning of our vacation, hours before we'd have to leave the beach and head for snow-capped mountains, my husband and I took off for one final walk in the sand. We urged our daughter to come along—the chance to say good-bye to the ocean and find that last perfect shell. But she declined. She was sleepy and grumpy and never one to make transitions very easily. Leaving sun and sand for school and routine was not a happy prospect for her. So we left her with her grandmother, content to watch something very silly on one of the several hundred cable channels that find their way to retirement communities all across Florida. She barely looked up when I called good-bye.

After our walk, my husband and I took mugs of coffee and sat in the sand near a short cement pier. The sun was brilliant, the sea calm. A few people in ice cream–colored swimwear picked through the morning's yield of low tide shells. But mostly the beach was empty and still. I was lost in thought about how to pack wet swimsuits, a smelly dead crab, and about ten pounds of shells when my husband gasped and pointed out to the horizon. He told me to hurry and look—he'd spotted dolphins swimming close to the pier. Sure enough, three or four dolphins dipped their graceful fins right in front of our eyes. I got up and ran for the pier, wishing I had a camera, but most of all wishing my daughter was by my side to witness this unexpected gift. *Why had she chosen Nickelodeon over this?!*

Tears rolled down my face as I watched the dolphins swim by. I knew that native cultures believe dolphins to be a harbinger of good luck, and I felt lucky and blessed and very alive as I stood on the pier holding my breath. But my heart ached that my daughter had missed it, she who had waited patiently for two hours on a tourist tug with her binoculars poised. Within forty-five seconds the spectacle was over, the dolphins gone from sight. But throughout that suspended slice of time, I had experienced two wildly conflicting feelings: life is beautiful, life is so incredibly unfair.

I told my husband that maybe we shouldn't even tell our daughter what we'd witnessed, to avoid the hurt we knew she'd feel. But we also grasped that to keep such a miraculous moment from her would be to deny something rich and important—the knowledge that sometimes, just sometimes, the universe provides for free in an unexpected moment what we think we need to buy tickets and stand in line for otherwise.

So, of course we told her, with a mixture of reluctance and triumph, trying to recapture the mesmerizing elegance of the beautiful creatures. And of course she cried, and fumed, and berated herself for choosing "a stupid TV show and missing my only chance to see dolphins!" I held her and smoothed her hair and tried to let her feel her grief without having to fix it and make it better. Which, of course, I couldn't—the crux of it all. I couldn't turn back the clock, couldn't lure the dolphins back, couldn't predict with any accuracy when she *would* have a chance to see any. Life is beautiful, life is so incredibly unfair. At school, at home, on vacation, my daughters and I are continually having to learn about life's choices and consequences and the relative unfairness of it all, and the fact that sometimes chance and pure good luck have more to do with spotting dolphins, or making millions, or having babies, or avoiding danger than we'd like to admit. Sometimes you decide to curl up and stay put and miss something dazzling. Sometimes you go searching for something dazzling and find nothing at all.

Right before we left, my daughter handed her dolphin watch rain check to her grandmother, sighing deeply. "I guess we won't be needing these," she said.

"There's always next year," her grandmother replied, the eternal optimist. "A year isn't so long, you know."

My daughter shook her head. "I don't think so. I don't think the dolphins like those boats with Christmas lights and palm trees."

Sitting in the airplane going home, I watched Natalie stare out of the small, square window, scanning the sky the way she had scanned the bay for dolphins. I don't know what she was looking for, but I could see that she was still disappointed, still mad at herself and the universe for missing her chance. I felt helpless at the sight of her sad eyes and defiant chin. But she is a brave and patient person, a girl with dignity and resourcefulness who will find her way out of shallow water and enclosed bays.

The very next summer, we were lucky enough to visit another beach. The first morning of our trip I awakened very early, before anyone else, and decided to go for a solitary stroll. Getting dressed quietly, I heard my daughter stir and asked if she wanted to come along. I was prepared to hear that she wanted to stay in the hotel and check out the cable television options, but she hurried to join me, throwing on shorts and sandals.

We walked along the empty beach, watching as the fog lifted and the line between water and sand became distinct. I was busy planning out the day ahead when my daughter screamed and stood frozen in her tracks. She tugged at my arm and pointed out to sea and then I saw what she saw—dolphins! Of course—dolphins. Seeing them wasn't part of our agenda, and so of course they appeared.

We ran along the beach in the foolish hope that we could

keep up with them, follow them the length of the coast, just to have them in our sights. We eventually gave up, stooped and winded, jubilant and humble at the same time.

Natalie wanted to hurry back to the hotel. She wanted to tell the others her morning news flash: if you want to see dolphins you have to get up early just in case. You can't be sure if you'll see any, but you have to get out of bed and go on the journey or you'll never find out.

And if you want a life comprised of raising your children and pursuing your creative work, you'll need to follow the same advice. You'll need to get up early and go on the wildest journey imaginable. You'll have to accept getting sidetracked and leaving things half-finished, because you know in your heart that eventually you'll go back and pick up the threads, once again. You'll learn a rhythm of living and being and doing and not doing that isn't modeled anywhere else in the world. Your heart will be broken and healed a dozen times a day, and fear will visit you in the middle of the night when you most need to sleep. You will doubt your path, and then the road will appear clear and welcoming. You will falter and stumble, and vow to give up— but then you'll go to Montana or see dolphins or finish your poem or watch your child play in the snow and you'll know you're living in the red hot center of an intoxicating life.

So here is my wish for you:

May you dance under a rainbow in your flowing purple dress.

May you feel big and invincible and full of life.

May you reach out to touch the trees with one hand while you're reaching down to hold hands with your own ones.

References

CHAPTER ONE

Roiphe, Anne. *Fruitful: A Real Mother in the Modern World.*
Boston, MA: Houghton, Mifflin, 1996.

McCall's Magazine Interview with Rosie O'Donnell by
Wendy Wasserstein. *McCall's*, October 1999.

CHAPTER TWO

Bateson, Mary Catherine. *Composing A Life.* New York:
Plume, 1990.

Jeffers, Ph.D., Susan. *I'm Okay, You're a Brat.* London: Hodder, Stoughton, 1999.

CHAPTER THREE

Lowinsky, Ph. D., Naomi Ruth. *Stories from the Motherline.*
New York: Tarcher, 1992.

Lazarre, Jane. *The Mother Knot.* Boston, MA: Beacon Press, 1986.

CHAPTER FOUR

Lerner, Ph.D., Harriet. *The Mother Dance: How Children
Change Your Life.* New York: HarperPerennial, 1998.

CHAPTER FIVE
Lamott, Anne. *Operating Instructions: A Journal of My Son's First Year.* New York: Fawcett Columbine, 1993.

Rosenfeld, M. D., Alvin, and Nicole Wise. *Hyper-Parenting: Are You Hurting Your Child by Trying Too Hard?* New York: St. Martin's Press, 2000.

CHAPTER SIX
Domar, Ph.D., Alice D. *Self-Nurture: Learning to Care for Yourself as Effectively as You Care for Everyone Else.* New York: Viking, 2000.

Rubenstein, Ph.D., Carin. *The Sacrificial Mother: Escaping the Trap of Self-Denial.* New York: Hyperion, 1998.

CHAPTER SEVEN
Borysenko, Ph.D., Joan. *A Woman's Book of Life: The Biology, Psychology, and Spirituality of the Feminine Life Cycle.* New York: Riverhead Books, 1996.

CHAPTER EIGHT
Tyler, Ann. *"Still Just Writing."* From *Child of Mine: Writers Talk About the First Year of Motherhood.* Edited by Christine Baker Kline. New York: Delta, 1997.

CHAPTER NINE
Richardson, Cheryl. *Take Time for Your Life.* New York: Broadway Books, 1998.

CHAPTER TEN
Csikszentmihalyi, Mihaly. *Creativity: Flow and the Psychology of Discovery and Invention.* New York: HarperPerennial, 1996.

CHAPTER ELEVEN
Lowinsky, Ph.D., Naomi Ruth. *Stories from the Motherline.* New York: Tarcher, 1992.

COLEEN HUBBARD is the mother of three daughters and the author of more than a dozen books for children and young adults, including the *Dog Tales* series. She is also a playwright, and her works have received staged readings at such theatres as the Oregon Shakespeare Festival, The Cleveland Playhouse, New York's Ensemble Studio Theatre, and many others. She has taught writing and drama to both children and adults, and speaks on topics concerning women, motherhood, and creativity. You can visit her Web site at *www.bigpurplemommy.com.*